Advance Praise for *Fire Your Boss*

"This is a seductive, subversive, practical book that could very well change your life. Leap!"

— **Seth Godin**, author of *This Is Marketing*

"Knowing what to do is easy, *doing* it is hard. This book will provide you with the courage to take action on long-ignored dreams, whether big or small."

— **Carl Richards**, *New York Times*
Sketch Guy Columnist

"Every decade I discover a few remarkable books. *Fire Your Boss* is one of them. This winsome book is brimming with wisdom, filled with hope, and is a sure path to reclaiming a life worth living."

— **Morgan Snyder**, author of *Becoming a King*

"I wish I'd had *Fire Your Boss* when I was forty. I would have devoured it line by line, word by word. And then, alone, I would have screamed at the top of my lungs, 'But where's the answer?' It's there dear reader, I promise."

— **Shawn Askinosie**, author of *Meaningful Work* and founder of Askinosie Chocolate

"Rich in wisdom, authenticity, and inspiration, *Fire Your Boss* paves the way for how to think differently and how to get out of your own way. Whether it's developing your own agile regimen or thinking in emotional currency, *Fire Your Boss* empowers each of us to step into our next level of leadership, from the inside out. Recognize the patterns that keep you stuck, and instead of quitting your job or settling for less, pause, and read this book!"

—**Rachael O'Meara**, author of
Pause: Harnessing the Life-Changing Power
of Giving Yourself a Break

"Aaron leads us into learning to be curious, remembering how to play, and aspiring to be more childlike, which have become key components in my own attempts to live more adventurously every day."

—**Alastair Humphreys**, author of
My Midsummer Morning and a National
Geographic Adventurer of the Year

FIRE YOUR BOSS

Discover Work You Love
Without Quitting Your Job

AARON MCHUGH

Post Hill
PRESS

A POST HILL PRESS BOOK
ISBN: 978-1-64293-080-1
ISBN (eBook): 978-1-64293-081-8

Fire Your Boss:
Discover Work You Love Without Quitting Your Job
© 2020 by Aaron McHugh

This is a work of nonfiction. All people, locations, events, and situations are portrayed to the best of the author's memory.

Post Hill Press
New York • Nashville
posthillpress.com

Published in the United States of America

To Leith, Holden, Averi, and Hadley.

Your lives give me courage, love, and joy to keep going.

CONTENTS

INTRODUCTION

THIS IS THE THIRD time I've written this book. The first version was a rant. The second was a passionate sermon. And this one is a swan song. I've contemplated quitting and not finishing this version a thousand times, but I knew you were out there waiting for a lifeline. The work you do every day is meant to make a lasting dent in the universe, but some of you don't believe it anymore, and your heart is growing weary.

I suspect you picked up this book because of the polarizing title, and you are banking on me giving you some silver-bullet advice on how to rid yourself of a boss forever. Sorry, pal, but this isn't a book about becoming an entrepreneur or about how to retire early. I'm offering alchemy. This is a book about how, in the day-in-and-day-out of going to work, you can learn to create irrefutable value in every workplace, regardless of circumstances.

If we attempt to tackle our career challenges head-on, Albert Einstein promises: "No problem can be solved from the same level of consciousness that created it." But if we take a personal transformation approach of becoming the kind of person who can move from fear to freedom, blame to accountability, disengaged to engaged, powerless to empowered, compartmentalized to whole-hearted, and rule follower to heretic? Well then, everything can be different.

Fire Your Boss is a new, liberated way of working where we learn to lead and manage ourselves, mature into wholehearted humans, and transform our work organizations from the inside out. True career liberation is an inside job. Always.

Together we are starting a revolution, a gathering of ruck-us-making, brave souls who share a conviction about the importance of doing work we love while engaging our heart, body, mind, and soul. In other words, we want it all. We're about to embark on a journey, a road less traveled, to confront the root causes fueling our workplace unrest. But full disclosure—it isn't going to be what you think. This is not a revolution with pitchforks and torches. As I said, this is an inside job.

Ready? Let's go.

CHAPTER 1

THE BIG IDEA

I was looking for an answer.
It's the question that drives us, Neo.
It's the question that brought you here.

—Trinity, *The Matrix*[1]

"I'M GONNA FIRE HER ass!" That's what I blurted out in a weak moment of heightened frustration. I was at my wit's end. Actually, I was beyond it. I'd tried everything: persuasive monologues, written business cases with colorful charts. I'd even hired outside consultants to help me advocate for the change I believed our business needed. But she was having none of it. No matter how compelling my pitch, she always held the veto power—and she never failed to use it. I knew there had to be a better way to secure the support I needed, earn the respect I thought I deserved, and gain permission to get the right things done. Yet, increasingly,

I couldn't contain my frustrations, and the negativity from my Monday-through-Friday work wranglings started infecting the rest of my life. I was ready to make a change. I was ready to declare my independence. I was ready to stake a claim on my future.

So, in the middle of another manic Thursday, I checked to make sure the coast was clear, then snuck down behind the bushes outside my boss's corner-office picture window. There I scooped up dirt and filled my World War II-era aluminum canister. Once safely back at my desk, I took a black Sharpie marker and labeled the canister with the company address. With my heart still pounding, I sat back with a triumphant smirk, knowing this was the beginning of my ability to move away from fear and to discover my well-deserved career freedom.

The dirt-in-the-canister idea had come to me while watching the opening scene of *Saving Private Ryan*. As the Allies stormed the beach, Sergeant Horvath carried a satchel of souvenir soil samples marked "Italy" and "Africa" from his successful beachhead assaults. When the D-Day bullets ceased whizzing by, he stuffed a fistful of Omaha Beach sand into a new canister labeled "France."

That sounds ridiculous, doesn't it? Scooping dirt out of my boss's flower planter. But at the time, I held tightly to old Hippocrates's words: "Desperate times call for desperate measures." Outwardly, my career looked successful, but inwardly I was restless and longing for something I couldn't yet articulate. On LinkedIn it would've appeared that I was happily ascending the corporate ladder, and gaining influence along the way. I was leading a small team of software developers in the creation of an application that oil companies could use to price retail gasoline. I like to explain our work as similar to the movie *Moneyball*. Billy

Beane, GM of the Oakland Athletics, brought math and science to the hundred-year-old game of Major League Baseball and revolutionized it forever. Our team did something very similar with the century-old retail gasoline market. We spent eight years creating and integrating science and technology into a solution for optimizing the best price for total profit and volume for each location across the globe. It's why you might see the price of gasoline differ by two cents between two competitors on the same corner. The work itself was exhilarating and innovative, but the company we worked for was quite challenging.

The most illustrative story to help you appreciate the extreme frustration I was experiencing is reflected in this single quote from my boss and CEO: "People are like aluminum. When you need more, you go buy them." What she meant was that people are cheap and readily available.

Without launching into a hundred reasons to refute her viewpoint, I'll just say that, as allies in this revolution of firing your boss, I know you appreciate how this type of thinking could create a difficult work environment (ahem).

My story continued with great expenditures of emotional energy spent arguing with owners over my bonus payment while I reached into my wallet to pay for new office chairs for my employees. The company line was that the one with a broken wheel would be "fine, just fine."

Unclear to me at the time was the reality that I was inwardly ruled by fear and dogged by the inner voice of self-preservation. You know, that authoritative monologue that convinces us to resign our will, silence our opinions, mute our creativity, and stifle our passions in exchange for safety and predictability. That voice would tell me:

"It's fine. I can take it."

"Tomorrow will be better."

"Just put your head down and get it done."

"You're making a mountain out of a molehill."

Yeah, you know that voice too, right?

I'm betting you've experienced your own version of this tension of survival and doing what is required of you—that sense of toeing the company line for someone else's benefit. Unfortunately, the corporate world has its unfair share of people feeling like—and being treated like—cogs in a very cold machine. But, like you, I accepted the tension, the frustration, and the disappointment as an expected part of the package of going to work.

You have stories in which the work you do, the environment you work in, the people you work with, the company message you carry, the customers you serve, and the product or service you deliver fall short of your original vision for how you'd be spending one-third of your adult life. So why do we do it?

Self-preservation.

We have bills to pay and families to feed. And by nature, we humans are resilient and adaptive, so we convince ourselves to stay at jobs we don't love, work with people we don't enjoy, in environments we know are toxic. Ever so subtly we listen to our fear and tune out the pulsing reverberation of our internal compass trying to point us in a different direction.

For many, work becomes the battleground of a thousand deaths. Others slowly grow deaf to their internal compasses screaming for a course correction with each incongruous intersection of their values and actions. Eventually, they shift into a coasting gear of apathy and disengagement.

I promise I'm not trying to depress you. But I also don't see any value in tiptoeing our way into the topic we have to cover: firing your boss.

Back when I was scooping a soil sample out of my boss's flower planter, I lacked the language and maturity to express the higher truth that lay beyond my defiance. Yesterday over a phone call a friend asked me, "Did you know what you were trying to accomplish in the flower bush that day?" With the benefit of hindsight, let me sum it up. *Happiness and contentment are an inside job.* My dirt tin was a symbolic first step of drawing a line in the sand and beginning to ignore the reactive voice of fear inside me. I'd decided to stop settling, and I started listening to my more creative beliefs and convictions about the way work could be. That moment marked the beginning of my quest to discover sustainable practices for staying engaged in my work, starting with the job I already had.

I've always believed that all of us are made to feel satisfaction in meaningful work, and underneath my soil-scooping Hollywood reenactment was the desire to rediscover a healthy life. On an even bigger scale, despite my daily reality, I've always believed that I'm uniquely qualified to make a lasting contribution to the future of work.

With that kind of an outlandish claim, you might expect me to whip out my long list of educational degrees from Ivy League institutions and experiences, starting with my first job out of college working in Washington, DC, for a presidential candidate. Neither of which is true. My pedigree qualification to positively impact the future of work is that I recognize patterns—invisible human patterns, which elude many people. Over decades, across industries, and at countless companies, I've witnessed humans just like you and me wrestling to find purpose, joy, and remain engaged in their work. In small and big ways, I've always felt a sense of responsibility to be a torchbearer illuminating the path to a more fulfilling way to experience work.

I didn't know how I was going to find joy in my work again, but I couldn't shake the voice of my inner heretic convincing me there was a *BETTER WAY* to work. Still, my daily workplace reality showed no signs of any lasting impact on the world. It was full of seemingly insignificant morsels, like taking lunchtime runs and showering in a mop closet or debating unsuccessfully with my boss over the lunacy of researching three price quotes for purchasing paperclips. My own daily career narrative appeared bleak. I now appreciate how those moments were the training ground for profound transformational shifts in the ways I began to reframe my engagement at work.

The Big Idea: "I'm Going to Fire My Boss"

I'll admit, I've always been a ruckus-maker. In school, I was that kid who felt the need to constantly ask the challenging questions: "Why do we have to do it that way?" or "Why does that rule exist?" and "Why can't we do it this way?" As I've matured, I've come to appreciate how much frustration I caused along the way. Yes, my high school principal was wrong when he told me in a closed-door confrontation, "You'll never amount to anything." But his frustration was warranted—I'd just dumped Palmolive dish soap into the biology fish tanks and, along with my classmates, watched straight-faced as suds spilled out of them and the fish bobbed belly up. I'm the first to admit that I haven't always made a ruckus for the right reasons.

But standing at that flower bed, I knew it was *the moment of truth* for my career—a worthy cause warranting a ruckus-making response. It was bigger than turning over my boss's veto power or spitefully winning arguments. This was the pivotal moment when I took ownership of my soul-level health and happiness.

"Fire your boss" became my metaphor for transitioning from a career ruled by fear, protection, and compliance to one of authoring my own operating manual for sustainable workplace engagement and high performance regardless of my circumstances.

As I write this, I'm nearly a decade beyond those neurotic moments of frustration and angst. I wish I could gift you with a single download of everything I've learned—to transform you immediately into the kind of person who can wield this new power. The problem is, information isn't as potent and permanent as transformation. I don't want to rob you of the growth and joy that will come through the struggle of creating new muscles, adopting new creative mind-sets, and fundamentally changing your beliefs about your career. It's the culmination of that process that brings the ability to fire your boss and to roam the spacious open places of freedom and creativity. (Can I get an amen!?)

If that is what you're seeking, there's a good chance you've picked up other career-help books. If so, you've probably found heavy tactics and dense prescriptions and repeatable formulas: "Do this. Start that. Create something, and you will crush it." This isn't that kind of book.

My friends, you don't need more shit to do or tactics to employ—you need a heart and mind-set transformation that shifts your root perspective about what's possible in your career. To that aim, I will share stories and scenes with you that represent my own transformational journey to a joy-filled, sustainable career. When I write "joy-filled," I'm not talking about zip-a-dee-doo-dah endless bliss—that's not reality. I'm referring to your work being undergirded by a deep purpose and meaning that will help get you out of bed every day.

Show Me (An Empirical Data Point for My Analytical Readers)

Some of you data nerds probably aren't sure what to make of all this heart-and-soul talk, and you need some empirical evidence showing why the status quo corporate culture is bad for us. All right, as you wish. Gallup, a management consulting firm, is the authoritative researcher on employee engagement and well-being. They define engaged employees as *"those who are involved in, enthusiastic about, and committed to their work and workplace."*[2]

The hard data from Gallup's well-being index reports that difficult work environments and our experiences in them can negatively influence our personal wellness and health. *"Research that has looked at the relationship between workplace engagement and health issues over time has found substantial connections between employee perceptions of the work environment and various health problems such as coronary heart disease, inflammation, and depression."*[3]

We're not crazy. The bottom line is that misery and disengagement at work carry over into our personal lives and affect our health.

Coping with Our Incongruence

Recently, while I was leading a client culture transformation workshop in Texas, a participant spoke up to refute the importance of being engaged and passionate about the work she does: "I don't know why we are talking about engagement and passion. We aren't in Silicon Valley working for Steve Jobs. We're in oil and gas (which is not as exciting as creating the iPhone)." I find it fascinating the stories we tell ourselves to help cope with our incongruence—the gap between what we want and what we do out of obligation.

Objectively, no one truly desires to work in a passionless and disengaged environment, but so many of us find ourselves downgrading our expectations and neglecting our dreams to conform to our workplace realities.

Regardless of industry, role, and career season, the wisdom from the late Steve Jobs (a college dropout if you recall) serves as a treasure map for us to discover joy-filled work: "Your work is going to fill a large part of your life, and the only way to be truly satisfied is to do what you believe is great work. And the only way to do great work is to love what you do. If you haven't found it yet, keep looking. Don't settle. As with all matters of the heart, you'll know when you find it. And, like any great relationship, it just gets better and better as the years roll on. So keep looking until you find it. Don't settle."[4]

Now that your heartstrings are reverberating, singing back an echoing affirmation of, "Yes, that's what I want," let's break down Steve's inspiration to extract and absorb his wisdom:

1. Because your work will fill up a large part of your adult life, it is too important and too pivotal to your life for you to be disengaged.
2. The only way to be *truly* satisfied is to do what you *believe* is great work. Only you will know when you are satisfied; no one else can define that for you.
3. You have to love what you do. You'll never be truly satisfied if love isn't driving your work.
4. If you haven't found work you love, keep looking and *don't settle*. Keep searching. Keep experimenting and exploring. Never allow the voice of self-preservation to convince you that this is as good as it gets.
5. Your work is a matter of the heart. As such, it cannot be solved by logic alone. It is not a linear equation where every step can be plotted; it exists in a more complex, deeper part of you. You'll know when you find it, and you'll know when you haven't. *Don't settle.*
6. It gets better with time like a best friendship or a happy marriage.
7. So keep looking. And in case you didn't catch it the first or second time—*don't settle!*

I prefer taking advice from successful people—those who have achieved or obtained something I desire. We can consider Steve

Jobs as one of our passionate, heretical guides on the importance of not settling, not giving up, and finding work that you love.

Before I found Steve's advice and Gallup's well-being reports, I too had become convinced that there is a path leading to joy-filled work. It starts with embracing the fact that being fully engaged and passionate about the work we do is critical to our own health, wellness, and career trajectory. Work is a blank canvas where you can choose your own adventure. Work can be life-giving, fun, creative, and challenging. Meaningful work isn't going to fall from the sky into your lap. You are going to have to find it and create it.

Unfortunately, There Are No Shortcuts

Not only are there no shortcuts, but the trail we're taking together is, unfortunately, the long way, with a signpost that reads "The Point of No Return." Joseph Campbell, the influential mythologist, writer, and lecturer, named this transformational detour "The Hero's Journey." Campbell says that no great story is a straight line from point A (something in my career isn't working) to point B (doing work you love with joy and vitality). Instead, every great transformational story—notice I'm not using the word *average* or *tolerable*—requires the hero (you) to go on a journey and face their figurative dragons (your internal and external fears) before they're prepared to wield their newfound, badass power and insight to save the planet and defeat the enemy. In this case, to kick ass at work while charting a life-giving course of being engaged in meaningful work and making a lasting difference.

Take a breath. Yes, you can do this. But it isn't going to be easy, simple, or fast.

Campbell promises that heroes experience a rebirth, but it comes after a descent to grapple with their fears. Think of Mr. Anderson becoming Neo in *The Matrix*, or Gandalf the Grey transforming to Gandalf the White, or, in more recent days, Carol Danvers facing her demons head-on to emerge as Captain Marvel. Here's a caveat: Not every hero succeeds. Some return home and continue the same humdrum existence they'd attempted to escape. But those brave few who stay the transformational course are reborn, equipped to face any challenge that comes their way. Take another breath. You can do this!

There are some requirements for your journey. You'll need an empathetic guide—someone who knows the way and has faced similar challenges (that's me). And there are two other critical elements: a willing heart and an open mind. That means you're going to have to try unorthodox things and break a bunch of rules of conventional wisdom along your path toward transformation. But if you're willing, the rewards will be worth it.

What do you think? Are you ready? A good first step might be to say it out loud, just to hear yourself say it. Get it out of your head and into the realm of reality: "I'm gonna fire my boss!"

CHAPTER 2

YOU ARE THE CAPTAIN

I am the master of my fate,
I am the captain of my soul.

—William Ernest Henley, "Invictus"[5]

LAO TZU WROTE, "WHEN the student is ready, the teacher will appear." Back in the middle of my depressing story, I felt stuck and trapped in my career. I was slogging through the frustrating hours, and it undoubtedly must have showed all over my being. I was more than ready. And, fortunately, one of my empathetic guides appeared.

After listening to a few of my depressing diatribes, a buddy gave me a copy of Hugh MacLeod's *Evil Plans: Having Fun on the Road to World Domination*. *Evil Plans* is like a Dilbert cartoon but with more irreverence. While occupying countless barstools in London, the author's accidental career began by sketching cartoons on matchbooks for patrons. Hugh's exaggerated satire argues that everyone needs an evil plan—a clarifying, higher purpose to get out of bed every morning. Picture Dr. Evil in *Austin Powers* on his quest for "one million dollars." Now, before you get nervous that I'm about to lead you into a life of crime and potential prison time, an "evil plan" isn't actually evil. It may seem subversive or threatening to the status quo, but that isn't a bad thing. For MacLeod, an evil plan is a funny way of describing a path for intentionally investing your greatest strengths in order to create some greater good. Oh, and happiness results as well. His heretic gospel crescendos with a promise: "You can wake up every morning feeling inspired and energized by the work you are going to do (that day)."[6]

This was just what I needed. Hugh helped me see that I was beating my head against the wall attempting to alter my boss's lifelong plan to be in charge and call the shots. The truth is, she never asked for help improving or revising that plan. She was perfectly happy employing minions like me to help her make another buck. I, on the other hand, was dragging my feet, feeling uninspired, and succumbing to depression. Without my own vision for a better tomorrow, I burned valuable emotional energy ineffectively trying to change my boss and my company.

In later chapters, I'll share with you a few zinger stories about the levels of dysfunction that triggered my internal ruckus-maker. For now, the point is: No wonder I was frustrated. I had big aspirations, but I was slowly losing my grip on hope.

Fortunately, Hugh was the heretic I needed to rattle my cage. His *Evil Plans* was the spark of hope that illuminated my reality and clarified these *big* realizations about my then-current gig:

1. The big spoiler alert is that help was not on the way. No one was coming to save me or hire me for the perfect job.
2. My boss and my company were not going to miraculously change. They were perfectly content with the current system. They were not going to wake up tomorrow, grow a conscience, develop a spine, or be visited by the ghost of Christmas past to upset their cart. They loved how things worked, and they had zero plans to make things better.
3. I was tired of my happiness being tied to outcomes I couldn't control. My only remaining choice was to reject the status quo, become the architect of my own rescue, and change my reality for good.

The Two-Thirds and You—Not Such a Good Scene in the American Workplace

The world has an employee engagement crisis, with serious and potentially lasting repercussions for the global economy.
—Gallup[7]

Gallup has studied US employee engagement since 2000 and repeatedly reports that roughly two-thirds of the working population is unhappy, disengaged, and not committed to their work or workplace. Globally, the numbers are worse, nearing nine out of ten. The polls say the average US employee's mind-set is to spend most of their time figuring out how to avoid being productive and just trying to survive their nine-to-five life sentence. In fact, those under age thirty-five are the least likely age group to say, "I have the opportunity to do what I do best every day" at work.

Sound familiar? Raise your hand if this sounds like you: "Hi, my name is (_____), and it's tough out here. I'm barely hanging on. I'm struggling at work. I'm simply trying to survive."

It's not that corporate America hasn't tried to make things a little better. It's that despite their best efforts to address our concerns, they've moved the needle only a little more than 1 percent.[8] Most companies attempt to solve the systemic decline in our workplace morale by improving management communication, the workplace environment, and authoring better mission statements. The sad truth is that companies by themselves will never cure this epidemic and have consistently failed at inventing an antidote to our pain.

Gallup's targeted inquiries drill into key questions like:

- "Does the mission/purpose of your company make you feel your job is important?"
- "In the last seven days, have you received recognition or praise for doing good work?"
- "In the last year, have you had opportunities to learn and grow?"

Good questions? On the surface, no doubt. We all want to be part of a mission we believe in, be applauded for doing great work, and develop personally and professionally. But there's a fatal flaw within Gallup's underlying assumption. We, *you and I*, are absolved from any personal responsibility, and 100 percent of the solution rests in the hands of our employers.

And this is where I'm calling BS. We need to take and remain in charge of stewarding our own happiness.

Taking Hold of Our Own Fate

The United States is the third largest workforce and the largest economy on the planet; yet, more and more, Gallup's results are camouflaging our real illness. Our disengagement is a byproduct of an undiagnosed infection of hopelessness.

Closer to home, you and I know that workplace stress is hurting *us,* not just the places we work. "Our sense of purpose, social relationships, financial security, relationships to our communities, and physical health are all negatively affected."[9] Some of us have forgotten that work is where we create art. Some of us have resigned ourselves to maintaining a passing grade (keeping the job), but we limit our efforts to merely delivering C- output (just enough to avoid getting fired).

Friends, what the hell are we doing here? We cannot allow this to continue. We are ultimately responsible for our happiness, our engagement, and receiving the recognition we desire.

If you're stuck on the treadmill of blame, apathy, and numb indifference, then I can help. I've got a tough pill for you to swallow, and I mentioned it earlier when discussing *Evil Plans.* Here it is: Help is not on the way. No one is coming to save you, least of all corporate America. And your company? It isn't going to change. But guess what? *You can.*

Don't think it's possible, or that it will really make any difference? Look at this silver lining in the Gallup data: one out of three employees actually enjoys going to work, gets promoted, and is challenged, rewarded, and empowered to craft a fulfilling career and balanced life. They do exist. Maybe you know one of the hopeful and empowered?

Sidenote to the happy one-third who are here with us: Hi there. I'm glad you're searching for new strategies to continually advance your career and solidifying a sustainable position of career strength and healthy work-life balance. Well done. As you probably know, our friends in the Gallup "I'm not sure how I can do this again tomorrow" majority need help. I flirted with becoming one of them until I discovered this unconventional path of renovating my career from the inside out. You give us a glimmer of hope that things can be different. And ultimately, we want to thrive as part of the happy one-third like you. That's the space where we're headed in this book, and together we will study life-giving, career-advancing behaviors and beliefs required for a joy-filled, sustainable career. And by the way, I'm confident that even though you're rocking your gig, you still need help creating an expanded toolbox of practices to go the distance.

Become a Heretic

Here's the deal: Everyone loves elements of their job, but the overall picture robs you of satisfaction, and for the fourth day, week, month, or year in a row, you go home unfulfilled at the end of the day. That's bad enough, but what's worse is, deep down, you feel powerless to do anything about it. Without a better plan, your strategy tomorrow is to wake up and give yourself a pep talk and then do it all over again. Before long, you're stuck in a repeating misery cycle, probably watching Not Suitable For Work videos at work and eating donuts with a fork.

We're better than this. But we all need a better plan. As the poet William Ernest Henley reminds at the beginning of this chapter, "I am the captain of my soul."[10] Our fate is not in the hands of our employer, our boss, or corporate America. You are the captain of your soul, and your prosperous tomorrow is within your domain of control.

So what's the plan?

Become a heretic.

Heretics throughout history—individuals like us—were the ones who rejected conventional wisdom and started revolutions to permanently solve their problems. A heretic is a person holding an opinion at odds with the accepted conventional wisdom.

When everyday heretics like you and me get really honest about their present realities and develop new convictions about a better tomorrow, history is altered. We have heretics to thank for the modern world that we enjoy today. Consider if our fellow rule-breakers had never hatched their own countercultural plans and envisioned a new world they wanted to live in. The flint rock of ideas always throws the first spark to light the torch of every revolution. Consider these examples:

Conventional Wisdom vs. Revolutionary Heretical Wisdom

Heretic	Conventional Wisdom	Heretic's Solution
Gandhi	Battles are won with guns.	Brokered peace by fasting.
Joan of Arc	Men lead troops. Women raise children.	At age 18, led French army to victory over England.
William Wallace	The biggest armies always win.	The army that fights with heart wins.
Martin Luther King	Black people aren't equal.	"I have a dream."
Oprah Winfrey	Men rule talk shows in America.	Keep your own name and ignore everybody.
Steve Jobs	Cheaper wins.	Design wins.
Mother Theresa	The poorest are beyond repair.	The poorest are closest to God.
Jesus of Nazareth	Caesar is God.	I am.
Walt Disney	Cartoons are for children.	Adults can become young again.

Heretics design a world they desire. They devise their unifying message and rapidly renovate their tactics, beliefs, and strategies for displacing conventional wisdom. Conventional workplace wisdom says: "We know you're not happy—we can fix it for you. Just hang tight while we spend the next decade seeing if we can budge the needle another 1 percent toward better." Heretics in the workplace say: "Here, hold my beer."

The conventional wisdom of our culture advertises two dominant solutions when you reach "I can't take this anymore." They say that to remedy your inability to experience a satisfying, engaging, and rewarding career, you either:

a) become an entrepreneur—because they clearly have all of the fun, enjoy the most freedom, and make tons of money,

or

b) discover your one true, lifelong passion that you were created for and then find a job doing that.

But there are tragic flaws with both of these conventional options.

As for becoming an entrepreneur, the reality is that eight out of ten businesses in the US fail within the first eighteen months and only 50 percent will survive the first five years.[11] And that "discover your one true passion" line? Do you know your one true passion? Seriously? What if it changes? That whole one-true-passion-to-guide-your-entire-career-or-life is a dysfunctional belief, according to Bill Burnett and Dave Evans, former Silicon Valley designers and professors behind the Stanford University Life Design course. They have studied thousands of students and concluded: "Many people operate under the dysfunctional belief that they just need to find out what they are passionate about. Once they know their passion, everything else will somehow fall into place. We hate this idea for one very good reason: most people don't know their passion."[12]

Conventional wisdom advertises a linear equation to success and happiness, but it leads to a dead end. Neither of its solutions fits you like Cinderella's slipper. But to do nothing means feeling stuck, disengaged, and uninspired in the same passionless career.

If we were having this conversation together over a beer, this would be the moment when I'd pause and hold the uncomfortable tension of our predicament. Then I'd say, "Friend, I found a better way. I cracked the code. I know how to destroy the Death Star. I uncovered the yellow brick road to Oz." There is an unconventional third way—a less traveled path where you keep the job you have right now but immediately begin renovating it from the inside out to discover:

- Freedom and autonomy
- Joy independent of circumstances
- More recognition and reward
- Less anxiety and worry
- Enduring optimism despite disappointing outcomes
- The confidence of becoming invaluable

You want to enjoy going to work every day. You desperately want to get your smile back. In the beginning, you possessed a powerful dream and vision for your career. I want you to experience a tomorrow that you direct, where you do work you love, offer your best every day, and tap into a rich vein of empowerment, hope, and creativity. I believe we share a fervent conviction that our lives and our work are part of a larger purpose. Work is the vehicle we steward to leave a good and lasting impact on the world. And there are sustainable rhythms between our professional and personal lives.

Yet we so easily forget that. Along the way, we lose sight of the desires and motivations that we held in the genesis of our careers. Somewhere, we began trading a day's work for a day's wage, and we lost the greater context of the story we are living in. But deep down you understand that you're made for more.

Welcome, my fellow heretic! I am inviting you to engage with me in the complete revolution of your career, not limited to but probably including:

- A mutiny
- A coup d'état
- A sudden overthrow
- A call to arms
- A fierce resistance to the old way

Don't worry. No one is watching you read this. I can sense you're not sure. Let me say it another way. You started your career as a heretic. Your ideas, beliefs, and visions were destined to reshape the world. But the hills got steep, the road got rocky, and hope is painful to maintain when you can't see the finish line.

Heretics never roll over and play dead while waiting for the world to change for them. They stand up, define the world they want, and start a revolution to realize their vision. We can be like our heretic brother Mahatma Gandhi: "Be the change that you wish to see in the world."

Now is the time to choose your path. Two quotes come to mind. First, Joseph Campbell: "We must be willing to get rid of the life we've planned, so as to have the life that is waiting for us."[13] And then one of my favorites from the great Morpheus of the *Matrix* trilogy: "Unfortunately, no one can be told what the Matrix is. You have to see it for yourself." Door number one will take you back to your cubicle and your old friends Apathy and Frustration. They will gladly welcome you home.

My invitation is to come with me behind door number two, beyond the life that seems planned for you into the one that's waiting for you. You can learn how to architect a career rich in empowerment, rewards, and choices. Liberate your career forever by joining this heretical uprising without becoming an entrepreneur, changing jobs, or white-knuckling your way to retirement. Discover how to plot a new course of career freedom to independence, empowerment, and self-reliance. I believe doing so will help you to find your smile again, rekindle your mojo, and start enjoying your work every day.

Be the change. Be a heretic.

Become your captain.

CHAPTER 3

DON'T QUIT YOUR JOB

After this, there is no turning back.
You take the blue pill—the story ends, you
wake up in your bed and believe whatever
you want to believe. You take the red pill—you
stay in Wonderland, and I show you how
deep the rabbit hole goes.

—Morpheus, *The Matrix*[14]

I NEED YOU TO commit. Raise your right hand and repeat after me: "I will not quit my job. I will stay where I am and renovate the way I work, where I work."

I don't doubt there are things in your workplace that need to be renovated. But for the moment, even if it feels counterintuitive, I need you to stay where you are. You don't need a new job or a new boss to be engaged at work. You need to learn to work differently.

In the previous chapter, we learned that, statistically speaking, two out of three of us are disengaged at work, that our workplaces are not going to change, and no help is on the way. And yes, in light of that, now I'm asking you to stay at your job. How does that make you feel? Seriously, what's your response to that?

When I came to the realization that I needed to stay at the job I had but reimagine the way I worked, I felt internally disrupted, and the old voice of fear piped up a defensive rebuttal:

- "How the hell am I going to work differently when this place stays the same?"
- "I have no idea where to start."

Maybe your response is similar. Here you are in the same job, the same cubicle (or lack of these days), with the same boss, and the same challenges. The temptation is always to believe that by relocating where we work, we can upgrade our contentment. It's some kind of variation on a theme of "the grass is always greener." I've changed jobs and careers a lot, and here's what I discovered.

After years of working for the same company, I believed there were no challenges left. The original zeal I felt for my job had plateaued to a tolerable "good enough." I'd find myself daydreaming, saying to myself, "I bet if I can get a job over there at Company X, I'd be excited again. Everything would change." Here's the naked truth: quitting our job will only provide us with temporary relief from another outbreak of the recurring rash of "I can't believe I have to do this for thirty more years."

Before we push the eject button, think of the hassle of brushing up our résumés, looking for a new job, going through interviews, evaluating the benefits packages, and comparing the compensation. And let's face it: The most significant gain in changing jobs is that we will restart the clock on a new set of challenges, a unique pairing of relationships, and a new boss. Quitting our job will not cure our deeper problem with contentment and engagement. The same internal baggage and unrest will surface again at our next gig.

Throughout our careers we all face challenges. Work is full of imperfect people, and we are guaranteed to encounter our fair share of knuckle-draggers along the way. But it's our own concerns, hang-ups, disappointments, and frustrations that detract from the joy and satisfaction we are capable of experiencing within our careers. Those who thrive in their careers have learned the necessary skills to navigate these predicaments. In one sense, they could work anywhere and be content because they've fired their boss.

Now to do that, you are going to have to face your challenges right where you are. But first, you need a greater awareness of how to approach your upsets.

You Are Wherever You Are

First, a little reality reminder. Your quest for career fulfillment is good, but you're never going to find the perfect company with the ideal boss, gazillions of dollars in compensation, a digital-nomad work arrangement, Ford Motor Company retirement package, traffic-free commute, impeccable coworkers, and a dolphin-saving, fun-loving, low-carbon-footprint, perfect-company purpose. There will always be imperfections of some kind. Always.

I've encountered many during twenty years of job changes. I've been through ten different mergers, acquisitions, buyouts, and hostile takeovers. I've worked for lean start-ups, publicly traded, privately held, and family-owned companies. I've gained and lost stock options, traveled globally, navigated shoestring budgets, nonprofits, bankruptcies, cash cows, and venture capital-funded offices complete with game rooms and slushy machines. My personal favorite was where we didn't have a viable product to sell, but we had excellent Golden Tee Golf tournaments (tongue firmly in cheek). No matter the setting, my unmet desires and frustrations always resurfaced everywhere I've worked. Every time.

I've tried everything from reading self-help books, attending career-advice seminars, starting entrepreneurial side hustles, and even seeing therapists. Those solutions provided me with temporary relief, which I appreciated, but they never entirely alleviated my more profound unrest. I was following all of the rules and adhering to conventional wisdom, but I was still frustrated by the results.

I started observing a pattern. Every three to six months, something at work would get under my skin, and the same combination of frustrations would resurface:

- I didn't feel I had the opportunity to do my best work every day.
- I wasn't receiving the recognition I thought I deserved.
- I didn't feel encouraged or inspired.
- The company's purpose wasn't meaningful to me.
- I didn't feel valued.

Back at home, I had three little kids, a wife, a mortgage, orthodontist bills, a country club membership, and a bloated suburban lifestyle that fueled my financial obligations. I was the breadwinner, and I needed these jobs, but something in my engine room was misfiring. In a painful moment of brutal honesty (picture Morpheus and his offer of red or blue pills), I scanned my career archives and replayed the old tapes to myself. At every job, frustration, disappointment, and powerlessness ultimately surfaced in the storyline, regardless of who my boss was and whether she or he was good, bad, or ugly. It didn't take a data scientist to conclude that it wasn't a coincidence that after fifteen different jobs, at various companies, under different bosses, I eventually arrived at the same conclusion: "I won't find happiness and fulfillment here. It must be over there."

To be fair, I've worked with some fantastic companies and for some extraordinary people. Even during those great seasons, I'd eventually ruminate on the lack of nirvana. I'd move on to the next gig believing, "Finally, I'll be happy." I'm also a world record holder for surviving multiple life sentences working for a couple of miserable human beings. I can't lie, though; hardship did become an excellent teacher. In later chapters, I will teach you how not all struggle is terrible and how to judo-move difficulty into something useful.

A few years ago, I had a conversation with my friend Morgan after I returned from a Hawaiian vacation. He asked me the typical questions: "How was it? What did you do? Did you enjoy yourself?" I paused and shared with him my disappointment: "I've realized the problem with vacations is that I go with me." What I was saying was, even in Hawaii (paradise, for God's sake), I'm still the same tightly wound, type-A, driven and over-caffeinated person. Although I had visions of long walks on the beach at sunrise with my wife, I opted for running alone in the morning to get in my workout. I brought a couple of books believing that in the land of aloha, I'd lounge in a hammock and lazily turn the pages between waves crashing. I never cracked open the books, and I don't remember any beachside catnapping. Nothing changed because I went to Hawaii. I showed up to vacation the same person I was at home, which didn't make for a very restful holiday. I operated the same way in both environments. At home, I believed the reason I couldn't relax was that I needed to go on a vacation to Hawaii. I learned that to rest in Hawaii, I had to become the kind of person who can permit myself to rest in my daily life.

The same is true for us at work. Who we are internally will find expression externally in every workplace environment, every job, and every meeting. The solution isn't to relocate to another company—it is to renovate ourselves so that it's our best version showing up no matter the environment.

Here's the red-pill reality that eluded me for fifteen years: It became increasingly evident that concurrent with the imperfections in my companies and bosses…wait for it…*I* was also part of the problem.

Once more for those in the back: "I was also part of the problem."

Before this *aha!* awakening, I was utterly convinced that across every job, every company misalignment, every Michael Scott-like boss, every coworker disagreement, every difficult customer—"they" (the captains) were mysteriously responsible for every bad day.

Friends, the sobering reality I discovered was that I was an accomplice, a supporting actor, and a second-in-command to every disappointment, shortcoming, frustration, conflict, and upset career story.

So I chose to stay. I decided to work where I was. I determined to become my own captain. Quitting my job wasn't necessarily going to help me. Quitting your job isn't your solution either.

Feel free to put the book down and take a walk around the block, or do some burpees, or maybe even treat yourself to some chips and salsa, and give that power punch a think before moving on.

If/Then Becomes Because I Am/I Will

Like believing *if* I could just get to Hawaii, *then* I would rest, I thought *if* I could just work somewhere that rewarded me, *then* I would be more innovative, creative, and authentic. No doubt we are highly influenced by our environment, and we can choose to be innovative, creative, passionate, and inspired regardless of our situation. But here's a simple framework that I believe we easily default to using, even though it's rooted in powerlessness:

*If*_____ *then*_____.

- *If* my boss inspired me, *then* I would be more innovative.
- *If* my company weren't so rigid, *then* I would be
  more creative.
- *If* my environment weren't so impersonal, *then* I would be
  more authentic at work.

If/then is called conditional thinking. These imperfections—"My boss doesn't inspire me...My company is inflexible...This place is so impersonal"—build our case for aborting. Convinced by these negative reasons, we validate our disengagement, frustration, and disappointment and fall into the pit of powerlessness, convinced that if the conditions were just different or right, then life would be different and better.

But what if there is another way?

"I quilt"

When you've had enough, can't tolerate your job any longer and are ready to quit, perhaps you could try one last thing.

Quilt instead.

You've got nothing to lose, right? I mean, you're going to quit anyway, so what's the worst that could happen to you?

So quilt. Spend hours every day integrating the people you work with into a cohesive group. Weave in your customers as well. Take every scrap, even the people you don't like, and sew them together. Spend far less time than you should on the 'real' work and instead focus on creating genuine connections with the people you work with. Including your boss. After all, once you quit, you're never going to see them again anyway, right? Might as well give it a try.

> *Careful...it might change everything.*
> —Seth Godin[15]

Godin's quilting analogy can equate to a very different operational framework that looks like this:

BECAUSE I AM/VALUE _____,
I WILL _____.

- BECAUSE I VALUE authenticity in relationships, I WILL engage authentically with people at work.
- BECAUSE I VALUE being creative, I WILL offer my ideas freely.
- BECAUSE I AM passionate about people being engaged at work, I WILL host a brown bag walking lunch for coworkers to talk about how we can offer our best.
- For now, you can't quit. There is a lot of meaningful work to do where you are. Instead of leaving, you can start doing everything you would've done at your ideal new job where you work today. Instead of continuing to blame, you can own your contribution to your disengagement and lack of synergy and see the upside of engaging differently. You can I *am*/I *will*.

What does that actually look like? This recent conversation with one of my coaching clients illustrates it well. He was convinced that he needed to change careers from engineering to working full time at a church. His reasoning was that in order to make a real impact in this world, he needed to help people with life's deepest challenges.

Me: "How do you know if you are any good at helping people with their problems?"

Him: *Silence.* (He wasn't sure how to respond.)

Me: "I mean, you're talking about quitting your ten-year career and going back to school to then hopefully get hired at a church. That sounds like a big risk. Have you ever tried listening to your coworkers about their life challenges?"

Him: "Not really. My company doesn't work like that."

Me: "Well, you're going to quit anyway, right? Why not run a little experiment and start acting like a pastor right where you are?"

Two weeks later, he reported back that he had taken the risk, broken his perceived rules of workplace protocol, and had a couple of meaningful interactions with fellow engineers. He didn't quit his engineering job. Instead, he chose to be the same caring person at work that he is at home. He took the red pill, captained up, started living I *am*/I *will*, acknowledged his culpability in his dissatisfaction, and began quilting one conversation at a time.

We possess the same I *am*/I *will* opportunity to stop waiting for permission to design our work experience. We don't need a new role, or to relocate to a new group or company. As heretics, we must start by defining who we want to be and how we want to work. Then we can begin living forward into that future state. The one-liner close is *Don't quit. Stay where you are, but engage differently.*

CHAPTER 4

LESSONS FROM THE LAIR

Lessons in life will be repeated
until they are learned.

—Frank Sonnenberg[16]

THE STORY GOES THAT one year the warden of a prison decided to give the inmates the opportunity to send Mother's Day cards. Of course, this was if they wanted to. Well, they did. In fact, the response was overwhelming; so much so that they ran out of cards. Evidently the chance to tell Mom "thank you" was something these men wanted to do. They simply needed the prompt. The story also goes that the warden figured he would provide the same opportunity for Father's Day, even ordering extra cards in light of the Mother's Day response. But that's where the two stories diverge, for not a single inmate took advantage of the chance to tell

Dad "thanks." Evidently, there were other words these sons wanted to say to their fathers, words not found in a Hallmark dictionary.

That story always causes me to consider the topic of bosses. Like great moms, there are great bosses out there, and we gush with gratitude for the impact they've imprinted on us. We cannot imagine our careers without their life-giving nurturing and fervent belief in us despite all odds. Where would we be without them? Yeah, for most of us, nowhere near where we are now.

I've had a number of such great boss-employee relationships. They have radically transformed the person, the professional, the husband, and the friend that I've learned to be.

Those world-class bosses are worthy of a bronze statue of their likeness erected on my front lawn. I know that for me, if it were not for one of my great bosses, I might still be handing out slices of pizza and free CDs to listeners at live radio broadcasts in the parking lots of car dealerships on Saturdays. That boss? Scott King. In 1997 he hired me, seeing past my lack of pedigree qualifications, and I catapulted from selling "zero percent financing this weekend only" sixty-second radio spots to cultivating a software sales territory of publicly traded companies and tech startups in the Pacific Northwest. I've got tons of other great-boss stories— tales of inspiring leaders who make it easy for us to jump out of bed and charge into the field. While I'm at it, let me give a shout out to my other best bosses: Kent Hildebrand, Kathy Valentine, Brenda Goodrich, Vance Brown, Bob Stein, and Kai Grunewald. I have you to thank for knowing what "great leadership" looks like.

Not long ago, I found myself in the back of an Uber thinking about great bosses, curious as to how frequently we should expect to work for such people. I decided to do some primary research and engage my driver, Rich. He was already five minutes into a reminiscent riff about his early career working in New York City's financial district as an auditor for a large accounting firm: at the office late, up early, and back again pounding out tax returns for corporate America. I asked, "Hey, Rich, throughout your career, then and now, what percentage of the time have you worked for a great boss?" He thought a second: "One-third of the time." Statistically speaking, Rich knew he was beating the odds of the universe, which included the company he was driving for that day.

I pressed a little more. "And what made them great?" I could suddenly tell Rich wasn't sure why I was asking so many questions about his job. He got a little cautious. So I went ahead and broke my cover. I told him I was writing a book about firing your boss without quitting your job. He relaxed a little and asked, "How could you ever do that?" I gave him the elevator-pitch version of the book. He smiled a mischievous grin, and I became his willing bartender, serving him liberating truth elixirs for the rest of the ride. Embedded in his stories of hall-of-fame bosses, three themes emerged.

- They trusted each other.
- They gave him lots of autonomy and freedom of choice.
- They established a mutual respect for each other.

The heartwarming footnote was that as they invested in him, they also took the time to get to know him as a person. Isn't that wonderful? I get choked up just thinking about it. I was tempted to strike this story from this chapter, but then I realized that some of you don't believe in the reality of great bosses, placing them in the same fairy-tale realm as unicorns. It's vital that you know there are good humans in the world in the form of great bosses. And for our inmate friends, I can vouch for the existence of great fathers too.

Life's Not Hallmark

But you know as well as I do, life's not a Hallmark card. Not even close. And this isn't a chapter about how to thrive under the care of a great boss. You don't need my help with that. Unfortunately, like difficult fathers, some bosses have left their mark on us. These could just be scuffs and scratches, but other times they are deeper wounds—a bruised self-confidence, a shaky resilience, or even worse, a cynical heart. Of course, odds are high that your boss today doesn't fit into the classifications of good or bad, but smack dab in the mediocre middle (which is almost worse). Your boss isn't causing trauma, yet he isn't improving your engagement at work or contributing to your growth either. He's just, well…there. Sorta like a wall.

Gallup affirms that the talent pool of great leaders is pretty thin. "If great managers seem scarce, it's because the talent required to be one is rare."[17] Their research reveals that about one in ten people possess the combination of experience, knowledge, and natural leadership that creates high-performing teams. A dismal outlook, as the probability forecast says that nine out of ten times we will work for a boss, leader, manager, or CEO who falls short of being great. Even if you're in the comfort of greatness today, change is inevitable based on the increasing rate of complexity in our world. This means you better get ready and build a new set of skills to navigate outside the safety of your comfort zone.

Look, early on I promised you that we'd have to go into the hard places, where the dragons live. This conversation about mediocre or bad bosses? It's the dragon's lair. But here's the deal. In all the great myths and stories, a dragon is symbolic of a challenge, no doubt, but also of a lesson or two. In other words, there are lessons here to be learned and savored in your ongoing quest. Failure to pay attention to them usually means encountering them again and, unfortunately, again.

Regardless of your boss's greatness rating, it doesn't matter. I'm going to repeat that for those of you in the back. It doesn't matter if your boss is great or terrible or mediocre; the way of freedom lies in paying attention to the liberating higher truth:

> *Every boss, good or bad, has an essential lesson to teach us, and the lessons get easier when we choose to become a willing student.*

Negative Examples

To illustrate, let me introduce you to one of my early teachers. I'd like for you to meet Mr. Cliché.

As part of an organizational restructure, Mr. Cliché was hired as our new director of sales. The restructure took me away from a boss that I loved, and I sensed pretty quickly that working for the new guy was going to be a challenge. At the time, I was young and green, only needing to shave on even-numbered days of the week. Unlike my great boss that I loved, Mr. Cliché liked to call sales plays in the comfort of his office, away from customers. He avoided the front lines with our customers and prospects, and opted for spouting off quotes he'd read from business self-help books. One of my all-time favorites (I can still recall it like it was yesterday) was: "Plan your work and work your plan." Now, what he said wasn't the problem. He was a nice enough and likable guy. Yet apparent to every one of us in the sales pit, he lacked the necessary emotional intelligence to know or care whether his advice was helpful or even applicable to the situation. My brothers-in-arms and I learned to keep him away from our customers and dodge his drive-by-sales-manager inspirational moments.

By the way, my assessment about his leadership value hardened like cement: "This guy is a dipshit." When my workplace frustrations began bleeding into my after-hours, I shot up an SOS flare, confiding to an older mentor: "Mr. 7 Habits is driving me nuts with his unsolicited empty advice. What do I do?" He helped me devise a plan to defuse my frustration and outwit every clichéd sound bite with humility and professionalism. When my arm-chair-quarterback boss would spout off, I learned to nod my head in earnest agreement, internalizing the original author's wisdom. It became a way to delineate my appreciation with the quoted author's golden nuggets. Then I'd either ignore Mr. Cliché's interruption and not respond to his book report, or I'd ask with genuine interest, "What book is that from?" Or, "Who wrote that?" As every good story should end, the villain was fired from the company before his second anniversary. His smoke screen was thick enough that it took a while for his boss to see past his ability to say all the right things. His MBA façade failed when he missed his revenue targets and his staff started quitting. His bad leadership from two decades ago instilled in me a profound clarity on the type of leader I want to be today.

Thanks to Mr. Cliché, I learned these leadership lessons:

1. Don't be full of shit and spout off stuff you read in a book. Become the kind of person who is full of wisdom and offers it when appropriate and helpful.

2. Lead from the front line with your team, not from the comfort of the command center. Get out and meet customers, roll up your sleeves, get down in the mire and muck, and only ask your team to do what you're willing to do yourself.

I'm eternally indebted to Mr. Cliché for the poor example he modeled for me. I learned what I *didn't* want to be and consequently aimed my leadership trajectory toward becoming gritty, relational, and leading from the bow of the boat, not the safety of the stern. I'll admit I did not have the maturity then to view my tour of duty with Mr. Cliché as a gift. That has come in retrospect. Only recently did I learn to reframe those negative examples into valuable life lessons.

The Mind Is Primary

Sunni Brown, a fellow revolutionary and one of *Fast Company*'s 100 Most Creative People in Business, once told me: "If you can't change your mind, it's very hard to change your life. Human beings that are mentally agile, those who can and will unstick—

from an ongoing challenge, a mind-set, a limiting belief, or a point of view—are more likely to flourish. Period."[18]

The fact is, we are going to work with and for challenging people. But these upsets can become setups for us to flourish. As Sunni suggests, we can exercise control over our way of thinking and loosen our grip on our limiting points of view, like: bad bosses are not just bad but useless. I think what Sunni means by "unsticking" is moving beyond, moving forward, reconciling, and not allowing our challenges to define us as human beings.

We can choose to take steps toward becoming mentally agile. We can be liberated from being stuck in negativity that restricts our ability to flourish in any assignment. That "mental agility" is very close to another quote that can be traced back to Mark Twight, alpinist, founder of Gym Jones, and trainer of such Hollywood specimens as Henry Cavill (Superman) and Jason Momoa (Aquaman): "The mind is primary." The mind is the most important muscle we have. Make up your mind, and the body will follow the mind. Don't make up your mind, and chances are good you won't be able to unstick.

It's Not Punishment

Listen, I'm not going to lie. If it were not for a mentor, I would never have "unstuck" from this "good vs. lousy boss" binary way of thinking. Not too many years ago, I was certifiably stuck, frustrated, and feeling trapped in the downward spiral of bad-boss powerlessness. I used a lifeline and reached out to a new friend with more gray hair than I had to hopefully help set me straight—

Greg Gilkerson, then CEO and founder of software company PDI (Profdata Inc.) in Temple, Texas. Our companies were technology partners, which in simple terms meant we had a technological ability that made our software solutions play nice with each other, making it easy for our shared clients. Greg is legendary in the convenience store industry. Thirty years earlier, he'd bootstrapped his back-office accounting software. He and his team created a company known for integrity, fairness, and quality.

I called and his admin patched me through. "Greg, can I fly down and spend the day with you? I'd like to ask you some questions about what it was like when you were facing some of the same challenges that I'm facing today." Then I heard the answer I'd hoped for: "Sure, Aaron. I'll clear my calendar. Just tell me when you want to come."

Greg was an open book. He brought in his executive team, introduced me to anyone I wanted to meet, and shared the juicy stories of how, for their first live software demos, his admin insisted on buying and wearing a red dress. I don't recall the exact reason, but I imagine if the software was glitchy, a pretty woman in a red dress provided a helpful distraction for the audience.

But the best advice Greg provided was, "Don't assume all hardship and difficulty is bad. Hardship is not punishment. It's more often the mission." He elaborated with a story about the anxiety he'd faced reporting to a new boss and how excruciating he found their relationship because of his boss's style of strict control and demanding nature. After this went on for years, he realized what this relationship had taught him: "Sometimes hardship and difficulty is the teacher."

That was truly an enlightening moment for me. Instantly, I realized that every great boss and every terrible boss I'd had thus far were equally powerful teachers and partnerships. When I've had a great relationship with my boss, miraculously, the rest of life seemed to have a lightness and ease to it. Flip the polarity scale, and it's been nearly impossible to be happy at home (or anywhere for that matter) when my working relationship with a boss was strained, complicated, and unhealthy. But both scenarios were classrooms with crucial lessons to be learned. At times it's beneficial to write some of this down. I've done it here in the form of a letter—sort of a love letter to the bosses who've forced me to wrestle. You might consider writing something similar to those bosses in your life.

Dear bosses throughout my career
who've enlightened me,

> *Yes, you know who you are. I wanted to let you know that your lack of positive role modeling, your poor relationship skills, your batshit-crazy control, unreasonable demands, and poor choices have all been a gift to me. A dark gift, no doubt, but a gift nevertheless, of examples (so many) of how not to be a leader. I'm savoring all this now, and it's good.*
> *Thank you for the trial by fire and the seasons of hardship and difficulty you provided. They all proved to be powerful apprenticeships that illuminated my road less traveled—the path I choose every day to not be like you. I can see clearly now that just*

as life revolves in and out of seasons, eventually the
time I spent with you came to an end (thank God).
I'll never forget you, and I'm forever in your debt.

Quite sincerely,
Aaron

Ahh, that feels good. I believe it is important to write that down and to say it out loud. I've found that doing so transfers the power away from those negative bosses and experiences and gives it back to me, where it belongs.

Not the Boss of Me

Finally, I want to pull in a snippet from my original unapologetic manifesto. It's a good way to cap this chapter, pivoting away from talking about our bad bosses and applying the lens to us, our motives, and our ways of showing up in the relationship. Because the truth of the matter is that in the relationship between you and your boss, they're not the boss. That's right. Your boss is not the boss of you.

Your boss does not hold the verdict on you. Your impact, your worth, your genius, and your workplace value is not in their hands. Far too much of your energies are consumed with interpreting your leadership's appreciation and acknowledgment of your contribution. It's wasted energy. It's wasted life.

After work, do you recreate your own version of ESPN's *SportsCenter*? Do you start running the B-roll film from the day, inserting your color commentary on the workplace play-by-play which all too often includes your incompetent boss as the star of the show?

Do your dinner table conversations and dates with your partner get chewed up with workplace drama? Again, not limited to, but mainly involving:

- What your boss said
- What your boss didn't say
- The resulting impact on you
- How you're not sure if you can take it one more day
- And how, if you were a millionaire, you'd tell your boss to take this job and shove it, then you'd go do what you're really passionate about

Yeah, I bet even your partner is tired of your boss.

Of course, all of us want to be noticed and appreciated for our workplace contributions. That's totally fair. But we put too much weight on whether our boss or company displays appreciation or gratitude for us in the way we desire. The fact that our paycheck comes from our boss and company keeps us at a heightened state of awareness. Left unchecked, we are prone to not operate fully from the healthy, centered place inside ourselves. So we succumb to internalizing our boss's feedback, or silence, as the verdict on our workplace value, and even more profound, our worth and value as human beings. Friends, this is not good. Not good at all.

Here are a few final lessons I've learned from the lair. I have learned them the hard way, and they have sustained me during long spells of struggle with my boss.

Stop doing your work for your boss. At a motive level, find your center and choose to operate from that stronger place. You can still adhere to deadlines, meet objectives, and fulfill your responsibilities, but stop doing it because you were told or required to. Make a choice that you believe in and, out of that empowered-spacious place, do your work because you choose to.

Assume the best. No news is good news. Head down the path you believe you should follow and assume the best outcome, assume everyone is supportive, and assume you are going to be successful. If someone above you has a problem with it, they will tell you so. Your idea is not good or bad as a result of the feedback you receive. If you believe you have a great idea, a worthy project, or the right decision, then go for it! Do it because you believe in it and because it is the right thing to do.

Consider the source. If you consistently receive negative feedback from the same person(s), consider that their negativity is likely a projection of their own inner turmoil. It took me a long time to realize that consensus building and democracy are not always useful. Some people will never be supportive or helpful. That is just the way they choose to be, and that is okay. Coach yourself with some inner dialogue. I've found the Al-Anon Three C's phrase very helpful: "I didn't cause it. I can't control it. I can't cure it."[19] Don't allow their negativity to stop you from doing your own great work.

Own your mistakes. If you make a mistake, say so. Own your shortcomings, missteps, bad judgment calls, all of it. Most everyone is appreciative and understanding when you say, "I made a mistake. I am sorry." This is also known as being a good leader.

Your boss isn't getting what he or she needs either. Yep. Your boss desires the same validation and acknowledgment that you do. And more than likely, if they are not giving it to you, well, chances are they're not getting it from their boss either. And yes, everyone has a boss.

Your boss is not the boss of you. You are. Realizing this one (and I continue to realize it) was a massive tectonic shift for me. Once I realized that my boss didn't have the verdict on me, I was free to do my best work regardless of their recognition (or lack of). Freedom is such a relief. I spent so many years attempting to gain the appreciation and confidence of leadership that I was exhausted. The truth is, it was like playing a baseball game with one eye on the game and one eye on my boss in the bleachers. As a result, I was never fully in the game because I was more worried about whether I was seen for the great plays I made. Now, I've learned to offer my best work every day and get my head into the game instead of spending so much time wondering what the commentators say.

I'll give Gandhi the last word(s) in this chapter. I cannot improve upon them. They are timeless and true:

> *Your beliefs become your thoughts.*
> *Your thoughts become your words.*
> *Your words become your actions.*
> *Your actions become your habits.*
> *Your habits become your values.*
> *Your values become your destiny.*[20]

CHAPTER 5

YOUR VERSE TO CONTRIBUTE

The question, O me! so sad, recurring—
What good amid these, O me, O life?
Answer.
That you are here—that life exists and identity,
That the powerful play goes on, and you may contribute a verse.

—Walt Whitman, "O Me! O Life!"[21]

YOU ARE MEANT TO rule the world. Okay, maybe not the entire world, but you are meant to leave a lasting mark on this world by contributing your verse to the ongoing play. Whitman's poem reminds us that we have a choice: either we engage our lives with gusto or we muddle through. Make no mistake—the invitation is for you to show up to your life, your work, and your relationships convinced that you have a vital role to play.

Recently, my wife and I attended an outdoor wedding at eight thousand feet above sea level in the steam-engine, Western town of Hot Sulphur Springs, Colorado. After the vows were exchanged, the music cranked up and the kids migrated onto the makeshift dance floor covering the wild prairie grass. A dozen kids accepted the invitational beats of the DJ, and one six-year-old girl had moves like Beyoncé. Another little girl dashed out of the tent, then returned wearing her brand-new astronaut jumpsuit with NASA patches and an aviator cap. Miss NASA's mom reported, "Yesterday was her birthday, and she wanted an astronaut uniform. She wants be an astronaut."

Little kids usually have a pretty good grasp on their desires and on simple questions like: "What's most important to you? And who do you want to be when you grow up?" Little Miss NASA went on to tell me about her dream of attending Space Camp when she turns thirteen. Her eyes sparkled as she told me about her dreams of space travel when she "gets big."

My Inner Eight-Year-Old

That little eight-year-old girl helped remind me that every one of us started with a dream. Maybe it was a dream of becoming a nurse, a TV screenwriter, an aviation engineer, an astronaut, or a lion tamer in West Africa. For some, it might have been curing diseases, or stopping bad guys, or becoming a mom and raising healthy children.

I think back to when I was eight. I wanted to be a marine biologist. I wanted to be like the red-beanie-wearing Jacques Cousteau, working with dolphins and diving the deep oceans in a submarine in search of hidden treasures.

When I was eight, I also loved riding my hand-me-down BMX bike. My brother and I would ride around town dumpster diving to collect aluminum cans. The stench and filth of the trash didn't bother us. Our town had a recycling program that paid a nickel rebate for reclaimed aluminum cans and a whole dime for a glass Coke bottle. With our black Hefty trash bag full, we'd pedal to Nowell's grocery store, collect our reward, and buy a box of Crunch 'n Munch caramel corn in hopes of winning the jackpot prize: a full-size Pac-Man arcade game. The dream of playing Pac-Man without ever again having to pay a quarter for three lives at the arcade kept us pushing through trash heaps. It was the motivation for our adventure.

When I was eight, I loved adventure and being part of a big quest—even something as silly as winning a full-size arcade game. Today, I'm not a marine biologist, but I'm still holding out hope for the day I swim with wild dolphins and sleep in a submarine. These childhood stories serve as anchors, reminding me of what makes my heart come alive. What was true about me then remains true about me today.

Mythic and Specific Truth

I'm willing to wager there was a good beginning to your career story. In the beginning, you had a dream, a vision, a target to aim toward. Your future was so bright. Before your life and career got complicated, before obligations got in the way, you had a dream that made your eyes sparkle. You had no concept of adult vocabulary like *reality* and *financial security*. Like Little Miss NASA, you were convinced that you had a necessary role to play in the world, a verse to contribute.

Whom did you want to become?

What difference did you want to make?

Whom did you want to help?

What changes were you destined to bring?

Your eight-year-old self is the best guide for your career fulfillment. I know some of you don't believe me, or you scoff at the idea of your inner eight-year-old running your life. But let me introduce you to a concept that will help as you as interact with the ideas in this book: mythic truth vs. specific truth.

Mythic truth is a way of thinking with a degree of magic and mystery injected into our lives, our interpretations, and our mindsets. *Specific truth* is fact based, linear, and rooted in cause and effect. The challenge is that specific truth limits our magical thinking by demanding that a truth be explicitly factual or accurate.

Allowing your idealistic, whimsical, sparkly-eyed soul to be your guide is a mythic truth. Now in my late forties, I see clearly how much effort and time I put into thwarting the leadership of my young guide by assuming that mythic kid's advice was too risky to follow:

> *That's not practical.*
> *They'll never understand.*

You need to grow up and do what's needed; it doesn't matter if you like it or not.

Specifically, I'm not suggesting that we ignore work ethic and responsibility to do what's necessary. I'm talking about concurrently holding mythic truth in one hand and specific truth in the other to create a dualism of truth.

Twenty-five years ago, shortly after marrying my wife, I had a conversation with my father-in-law (FIL). With a college degree and a baby face, I sat across the lunch table from him, facing the topic of "How are you going to provide for my daughter?" My wife, Leith, and I had just moved to Colorado with no savings or promising career, and we'd just finished volunteering all summer for a Young Life camp, taking high school kids backpacking. From FIL's viewpoint, our choices probably appeared financially irresponsible and dreamy. I did land a minimum-wage job selling tents and backpacks at a local outdoor retailer, but his questions regarding provision were fair and valid.

My father-in-law is a real salt-of-the earth guy who worked in the coal mines of Pennsylvania during the 1940s. He built his family's home himself, one paycheck at a time. They didn't have enough money to insulate the walls before moving in, so to keep warm they stacked blankets and shared beds.

I'm confident I didn't wield my response to his question with the maturity that I would today. Nonetheless, here's what my young guide said: "I want to provide but not work so much that I'm away from my family all of the time."

Understandably, FIL's gruff response was something along the lines of, "You better get over yourself and do whatever is necessary whether you like it or not."

Doesn't Come Easy

Embedded in my response was this tension of mythic truth and specific truth. I did need to provide financially for my family regardless of how long or hard I had to work. What neither of us knew at the time was that my verse to contribute, my dent in the world, lies within the tension of work-life balance. Even then I agreed with his specific truth, but mythically I've always believed there is a narrow path to be sought and found where work, life, relationships, and play can coexist in a sustainable rhythm.

Concurrently, the mythic truth I was attempting to convey was that I love my wife, and I want to be with her and my future kids. I don't want to work so much that I never enjoy the people I love most. I also need to enjoy the work I do every day so that my heart doesn't shrivel up and die.

Back then, I sensed a vague, if undefined, notion that those two truths could coexist. Today, I've become the kind of person who can wield the duality of holding a mythic truth while stewarding the necessity of a specific truth. I can buckle down and do what's needed *and* simultaneously steward mythic truths that transcend my specific circumstances and season of life. Admittedly, it has taken years of effort, trial, error, triumph, failure, and experience to live consistently in the balance. Most days, I'm still far from where I hope to be someday.

For you, my friends, be aware that developing this life skill of calibrating your career and daily work—of balancing mythic truth and specific truth—isn't simple or easy. I think it's a lot like mastering the art of fly-fishing.

After ten years of working the rivers and creeks of Colorado and Utah, I can usually catch at least one fish during each outing, but some days I still get skunked. I still aspire to the kind of artistry displayed by Brad Pitt's character in the movie *A River Runs Through It,* but I'm decades away from reliably interpreting and intuitively reading the water and understanding which fly is optimal for the conditions, season, and water flow. What worked great last week, thirty miles downriver, can prove ineffective on a perfect weather day. Perplexing as it can be, fly-fishing requires a similar depth of adaptability and willingness to embrace mystery. Norman Maclean, the godfather of fly-fishing literature said it best:

"My father was very sure about certain matters pertaining to the universe. To him all good things—trout as well as eternal salvation—come by grace and grace comes by art and art does not come easy."[22]

Such is the mystery of balancing mythic and specific truth, but the triumphs of hooking into the flow along the way keep pulling you forward in the process of firing your boss and finding your verse to contribute to the world.

My friends, you are here on the continuum of time, and the powerful play is happening. If you gave your young guide permission to speak, he or she would never ever support you spending forty to eighty hours every week disengaged and disillusioned.

Regardless of how you've gotten here, if you're in a joyless or less than fulfilling career, then it's time to reclaim the fact that mythically you are meant—designed even—to be more, do more, and contribute more than you are today.

To be clear, I'm not suggesting that every one of us is destined for external greatness measured by charts and history books: to become president of the United States, to be on television, win the Nobel Peace Prize, write a *New York Times* best seller, or walk on Mars. What I'm naming is the invisible subtlety of choosing to show up to your life and to work with the deep satisfaction of living true to yourself with a fully integrated heart, body, mind, and soul, uninhibited and moving forward to offer something valuable no matter the setbacks and shortcomings.

My Inner Four-by-Five Self

Last summer I experienced my tenth career merger and acquisition. A private equity group acquired the technology company I worked for. I knew right away that I didn't have the stomach for their conquest of turning big profits and selling the company again in a few years. I'd heard the campaign speeches before, and I knew that after thirteen years of solving the same industry business challenges I'd lost interest.

On my office wall, I have a four-by-five-inch photo of myself standing in the doorframe of a burnt orange and primer gray Ford cattle truck named *John Wayne's Horse*. I drove it to drop off high school kids at remote backcountry trailheads in the Weminuche Wilderness of Colorado when my wife and I were newlyweds, living at nine thousand feet in a twelve-by-fifteen-foot log cabin built in the 1930s. My face in this photo is bright, and my smile is full of adventure and deep satisfaction. This is my younger guide. I have invited him back into my life as a counselor to my career's biggest questions. He stares at me while I work and mythically dialogues with me. I imagine telling him in the flesh that I'm considering playing it safe: *I'm going to accept their offer and sign up for the private equity conquest. No, I don't love it. In fact, I'm bored and have difficulty making it through a week. I'd rather leave behind this software technology career I've spent nearly fifteen years creating—but I get paid a lot, and I'm not sure I can replace my income starting a new career.*

I can picture his jaw dropping and disbelief in his eyes. He looks ready to shake me. I hear him say, *Aaron. Bro. We can't allow this. This was not the dream. You cannot resign yourself because you're scared and uncomfortable with uncertainty. Don't you remember how we were going to go into the business world? People—not money— were always going to be the mission. What happened to you?*

Can you hear my younger guide reminding me of my mythic truth? We can lose sight and connection with our original dreams when real life happens, the road gets rocky, and our obligations shroud our visibility into those distant origins.

I took my inner four-by-five self's advice and started asking him to remind me of what we promised we would create together. In response, I wrote this simple sentence in my journal: "I want to align the work I do every day with the person that I've become." It seemed so simple—so lacking in business-school-how-to-change-careers strategy—that I was a bit embarrassed by it. I now see genius within the simplicity as I was holding specific truth and mythic truth simultaneously.

For now, I'm purposefully going to leave you in suspense as to how this portion of my story concludes. What's important right now is to understand that our inner guide remembers the promises we made to ourselves. Regardless of where we are in our career journey—just beginning or near the end—there is always time to pivot and correct our course.

Obviously, there is a spectrum here, but the journey begins by stepping through the door—even just getting a foot stuck into the door. The opening will become more expansive over time. Firing your boss isn't a one-time event, but a way of living and working, grounded in the mythic and the specific. Don't allow the magnitude of fear (*Oh shit, where can I possibly start?*), the gap of experience (*I'm twenty years into a career I don't love*), or the confusion of uncertainty (*I have no idea what I love or want*) keep you tethered to the status quo of disillusionment and dissatisfaction. It's okay. What's important now is that you begin reconnecting with your younger guide(s) and start listening to their advice without offering a rebuttal to disqualify or dismiss their ideas.

Firing your boss requires us to see our lives framed within a larger story and appreciate that our careers are a reflection of our beliefs about the world, the divine, and our contribution of a verse to the greater play. In the beginning, you were clear mythically on what difference you were going to make. It's time to reclaim even the smallest traces of those dreams.

Remembering What You Know

To help you flesh out this idea further, pull out your journal or fire up your computer and answer these questions. I'd throw on some soft music and find a quiet place to riff on these big ideas. The goal isn't getting the answer or figuring out what career field you should be in. Instead, you're going to focus on bending your ear toward your inner guide to remind you of a few mythic truths about yourself:

- *What has always been right about you?*
- *When you were eight, what did you dream about becoming?*
- *What movies did you love?*
- *Who were your heroes, and what did you like about them?*
- *When you started your career, what difference did you hope to make?*
- *What goals or aspirations did you have at the beginning?*

From experience, I know some of you may feel paralyzed by soulful questions. And yet others of you might have answers rolling out of your mind and off your tongue right away. These answers might be brewing in your mind, ready to burst out. Wherever you begin, remember that the goal is to search for clues about what is mythically true about you. To help prime the pump, I've provided a few example answers to help you feel more comfortable getting started. Note as you read through my responses, I am forty-seven years old. The movies I watched, the toys I played with, and the heroes I admired are contextual to the era of my formative years. Regardless of your age or career timeline, anchor these questions in your younger guide's developmental years. The real treasures are waiting to be discovered in the early era of your life.

What has always been right about me?

I've always loved anything adventurous where the outcome was uncertain and the journey held a promise of mystery and discovery. My integrity was important to me even when I was young. I've always been emotionally attuned to people, circumstances, and reading a room. Epic tales and underdog stories have always especially captivated me.

When I was eight, what did I dream about becoming?

I had this Fisher Price Adventure People set with two guys—Hawk and Joe. They had a canvas tent, four-wheel-drive Jeep, canoe, and sleeping bags. I imagined myself becoming like them, exploring the edges of wild places.

What movies did you love and why?

Star Wars: I loved that Luke Skywalker knew his potential was far more significant than the little story he started in.

Back to the Future: George McFly standing up against bullies forever altered his future.

Raiders of the Lost Ark: Indiana Jones ejecting from life's humdrum and traveling across the globe, piecing together frayed edges of treasure maps and lost legends to discover the truth.

The Breakfast Club: Teenage angst culminating in raw, honest viewpoints.

Who were your heroes, and what did you like about them?

Jacques Cousteau: He had a sense of wonder about the ocean that captivated me. He didn't seem scared or intimidated by the unexplored places underneath. The invitation of discovery was a more powerful force than fear of the unknown.

When you started your career, what difference did you hope to make?

I knew in my gut that there was a way to show up at work with a fully integrated heart and head. That it was possible for us to lead from the heart while simultaneously accomplishing big things. I knew that I was somehow uniquely qualified (although I had zero evidence to prove this theory) to carry one of the torches for the future of work. I've always believed that work is where our hearts and heads combine to create something magical.

What goals or aspirations did you have at the beginning?

I wanted to be in charge and run the show. I didn't want to be a follower but a leader. I've never had specific career goals like, *Become a CEO by age thirty.* I've always aimed for more abstract aspirations like, *I want to earn $500,000 a year while working part time.*

My Younger Guide(s) Synthesis

For me this exercise is incredibly helpful for fleshing out mythical truths about myself. The above responses, taken collectively, help provide a North Star collection of insights revealing that I've always loved

- adventure in wilderness;
- challenges and conquests over predictability;
- being a pioneer—trying something new or unknown;
- connecting with people on a heart-and-purpose level.

But that's me. I'm interested in you. Now it's your turn. So what about you? When you begin to piece together those mythic truths about yourself, what begins to come into focus? It might be faint at first, but I encourage you to stay with it and keep asking the questions and listening closely to your younger guides. Your part to play in all this is vital, of utmost importance.

You may contribute a verse. What will your part be?

CHAPTER 6

MERCENARIES AND MISSIONARIES

The mercenary posture will keep you profitable.
The missionary position will keep you on top.

—Mike Rowe[23]

TEN YEARS AGO, I accidentally became a professional mercenary—I started playing the game of work in trade for money. The money started rolling in as I earned prestigious positions like executive VP of sales and marketing with a seat at the big boys' table. At first, it was exhilarating. I was traveling the globe, ringing the bell to open the day's trading at the London Stock Exchange, and driving revenue up and to the right.

Each time I achieved a new metric of success, I received a promotion to assume more responsibility and organizational influence. I was so proud of myself—and simultaneously unsure how much longer I could keep up the façade of my endurance, resilience, and endless capacity. I loved the work. I was invigorated by our accomplishments. But I knew I couldn't sustain the pace, and the pressure of performance was becoming overwhelming and endless. I was regularly working twelve-hour days across global time zones and either on airplanes or conference calls fifty weeks a year.

One January, I remember receiving my W-2 tax statement, and it read $198,650.00. My first reaction was, *I can't believe I fell $1,350 short of breaking the $200,000 mark.* It took me a few days to move past my disappointment and reorient to gratitude and the realization, *Wow, I just earned more money than ever before, and I'm upset about the fact that I didn't hit some mythical financial milestone.*

One year, I tickled $400,000 annual gross income, but no matter how much money I earned, emotionally it never felt like a fair exchange of value for my energy expended. A pit in my stomach developed—not about the money I made but how I felt while I was earning it. Slowly, I'd disconnected from my personal purpose and my love for people while I kept marching to John D. Rockefeller's drumbeat for happiness and fulfillment: "one more dollar."

But what about at home? you ask. That's a fair question. At home, my nineteen-year-old son was in a drug and alcohol treatment center. My twelve-year-old daughter had died after a lifelong battle with her disabled body, and my wife and I were struggling to keep our marriage alive. Our youngest daughter was in middle school, and I was regularly missing her life's most important moments.

I know, I know—there are so many stories here to fill you in on. I'm sure your mind is attempting to process *son in rehab, daughter died, middle school daughter*, and *marriage on the rocks*. My honest reaction is that I wouldn't know where to begin to describe the despair we befriended and the hopelessness and anxiety we ate daily for breakfast.

In the context of my career, you can imagine how important "one more dollar" became to keep one nostril above the waterline. Each day, I viewed my life through the lens of survival. I was so tired. Even during moments of peace and rest, I expended most of my energy bracing and preparing for the next big wave to come crashing in. Our behavior, driven by "one more dollar," is the visible part of the iceberg sticking above the water. But below the surface are the personal stories driving our behavior, and those are usually infused with fear, worry, anxiety, and deep longing. I feared running out of money. I feared being unable to support my family's great emotional, physical, medical, and spiritual needs. I was afraid.

Maybe this doesn't sound like the stuff of a business book to some of you. But I'm writing a book about being human at work, and that begins with acknowledging that our home life and our work life should never be entirely separated. Even the best-intentioned of us can get sucked into situations that end up eroding our well-being and, ultimately, our souls. We end up becoming mercenaries. I promise to fill in more details of the personal can of worms I just opened, but for now, back to the story....

A Night to Forget (or Remember)

Every transformational story has a low point, and mine happened over a business dinner in London. My executive team was gathered in a private room of an upscale restaurant, drinking fancy wine and eating overpriced dishes, the names of which none of us could pronounce. Despite the luxurious setting, the conversation got heated, frustrations gave fodder to anger, and the whole evening went into a reactive spiral. The business-review-turned-conflict crescendoed with fists pounding on the table. I don't recall my exact words, but I'm ashamed to say they were something like this: "No, I listened to you, and now it's your xx@#*^%$ turn to listen to me!" It wasn't my proudest moment.

Tick. Tick. Tick. Tock. *Boom!*

I ejected myself from the dinner to walk the streets of London alone. I was soulfully lost and isolated five thousand miles from home. It took many weeks to put the relational pieces back together from that dinner meeting. That unforgettable night, my true self awakened, and I knew I couldn't keep pretending that I could continue as a professional mercenary.

Back home in the US, I realized I needed a friend who'd experienced what I was going through. Are you ready for this? I turned to Jerry Maguire. I'm completely serious—*that* Jerry Maguire from the movie. On point with Joseph Campbell's "The Hero's Journey" of facing our greatest challenges, Jerry Maguire became my guide, my mentor, and my figurative Obi-Wan Kenobi to show me what I couldn't see through the lens of my own life. I was too close to the details and too entangled in the complexity of how I got to this crossroads to find my own way out.

If you haven't seen the 1996 movie *Jerry Maguire,* here's an introduction: Tom Cruise plays the slick sports agent whose career implodes in a single afternoon. In the first three minutes of the film, we get the CliffsNotes of Jerry's life. He's spent years working for *the* most successful sports management company. He is fierce and suave, but he's also dying inside. After years of corporate ladder climbing, he's forgotten who he was and ignored what was initially vital to him. In his words, he had become "another shark in a suit."

Standing at a moral crossroads, late on the night before his corporate conference, Jerry reaches his point of breakdown—and most importantly, his breakthrough. As he wrestles through to the point of his great epiphany, he does headstands in his hotel room and unravels how he allowed his soul to corrode. He remembers the sounds of the game, the smell of the field, and the convictions of his younger self. He remembers the way things were supposed to be. And what do actors in a movie do in such a moment? That's right—they craft a manifesto. He advocates for an unorthodox shift to give more personal attention to the company's clients. He redefines his vision for the future of his company—and his own.

Jerry remembers the simple pleasures that drew him to this job after law school: "The way a stadium sounds when one of my players performs well on the field. The way we are meant to protect them in health and injury. With so many clients, we had forgotten what was important....The key to this business is personal relationships."[24]

As I said, Jerry didn't have a breakdown. He had a break-through. He hit rock bottom and there unearthed his original love of the game—the motivation fueling his career passion. Somewhere between the Super Bowl championships, World Series victories, Stanley Cup trophies, and ginormous bonuses and pay-checks, Jerry had neglected his personal mission: "to protect them (the players) in health and injury." His original motivation had been caring for the best interests of his players, but along the way he had sold out and begun playing the game for money. He'd become a mercenary, and he hated himself for it.

In the next scene, we see Jerry running 110 bound copies of his heretical epiphany and stuffing them one by one into his col-league's in-boxes. He titled it "The Things We Think and Do Not Say: The Future of Our Business." Jerry Maguire was alive again. He was back.

Jerry's mission statement makes him famous, but for all the wrong reasons. His peers smile and applaud as they make eye con-tact across the lobby while making sure not to stand close enough to catch the career-suicide bug they know has infected him. Soon, Jerry is fired and leaves the office with his mission statement in one hand and a goldfish—his only heretical recruit—in the other. To be fair, the cute secretary comes with him as well. She can't resist a man of principle.

Defining Terms

I want to quickly paint a word picture to introduce you to a per-sonal framework that has radically clarified my motivation for my career: Mercenaries and Missionaries.

At a very simplistic level, mercenaries are motivated by conquest, advancement, and rewards. They are paid to fight, to play, and to conquer the next hill. If there isn't money and victory involved, a mercenary won't lift a finger. The strength they wield is that they bring competence, rigor, and excellence. Their downfall is that they lack loyalty and allegiance to a deeper cause or purpose. As long as the check clears, they can remain detached from a reason or meaning behind their conquest.

Jerry Maguire's inner mercenary convinced him that big money and prestige were a fair trade for the white lies he learned to tell, the women he loved and left, and the sense of emptiness he'd taken as a constant companion. Sleepless and feeling isolated, Jerry's soul began rejecting the hollow rewards of the mercenary and remembering the origins of his missionary.

By contrast, missionaries are motivated by purpose, impact, and deeper meaning. Their strength lies in their character and compassion offered in the service of others. In order to get out of bed every day, a missionary needs a unifying cause, like removing trash from the ocean and shorelines (2.5 million pounds removed in two years by 4Ocean.com), eradicating poverty (UNICEF.org), or freeing children from sex trafficking (TheExodusRoad.com). During his dark night of the soul, it was Jerry Maguire's inner missionary who broke through the plastic sports agent veneer and endless bullshit to launch his rebirth. His younger guide, his missionary, reminded Jerry of the dignity of caring for his players.

My mercenary by himself is prone to—and has been known to—author my career narrative toward an arc of making a pile of money at any cost. If I were to leave my missionary to his solitary will, he would steer my career to a worthy cause and undervalue the benefits of a steady paycheck, health insurance, and a robust savings account to weather life's interruptions. In past seasons, I allowed my mercenary to be the engine, steering wheel, and brakes—I made lots of money but soulfully felt empty.

Pendulum-swinging away from monetary conquest, I thought if I found meaningful work, it wouldn't matter how much money I earned. I thought my deep sense of purpose would be fulfilling enough to surpass money's grip. Writing this, I smile on my younger self's inability to recognize the vital partnership of being part mercenary and part missionary.

Getting Lost on the Road to Nowhere

Back in college, I avoided taking classes at the Baylor University Hankamer School of Business. I laugh at this idea now, but back then I had a very naïve, black-and-white conviction about the purpose of the business school. I concocted a belief that post-graduation, young mercenary recruits would begin a forty-year transformation into ruthless, greedy corporate pirates. I remember watching my friends leave for their accounting and economics classes thinking to myself, *Those poor mercenaries—it's only a matter of time until they realize they're being trained to steal from the poor, pollute rivers, and capitalize on the weak.* Out of simplistic fear, I successfully dodged taking any business courses during my tenure at Baylor.

Growing up, I didn't know many business people. My neighborhood was full of blue-collar workers. My next-door neighbor was an entrepreneurial drug dealer, which didn't end well for him when my mom called the cops. The few professionals I knew were dentists and doctors. My mom's boss was a financial planner who served ten years in federal prison after he was convicted of stealing money from old ladies. Objectively, my sample size of professionals—much less professionals making the world a better place—was pretty small.

So my solution to avoiding a certain and eventual death of the heart was to become a missionary. I believed I had to become a full-time, vocational do-gooder.

In my first interview after graduation, I told my soon-to-be sales manager, "I can't work in sales. I don't lie, cheat, or steal." (In other words, I'm a missionary). His smooth response was, "That's great. I hire people with integrity and character. I can't teach people how to be honest. The job comes with health insurance and a four-month salary guarantee." My wife was four months pregnant with our first kid, and at age twenty-two, we barely had a plan, much less a Plan B. He hired me on the spot, and I began my journey selling sixty-second radio commercials to bars, liquor stores, and homebuilders.

I adopted this mantra to ground myself: "I live in a mercenary world, but I operate out of a missionary heart." I was determined to put people first, fiercely guard my integrity, and bring goodness to my customers, colleagues, and those under my care.

I quickly adapted as I learned the trade of the mercenary, but I retained roots in my meaning and purpose, reminding myself, "It's about the people, not the money." I gained a front-row chair to thousands of ways to approach business. And I began realizing that the distinctions between mercenary and missionary weren't so black and white.

Idealism has a way of being shaped by first-person experiences. I've had "missionaries" stiff me and not pay their bills, and I've met incredibly generous "mercenaries" full of integrity. It all came down to motive and character, independent of industry, beyond for-profit or nonprofit status. The individuals I esteemed most transcended those categories and embodied the best traits of both the mercenary and missionary.

Fast-forward two decades and, like Jerry, the workplace obligations and the pressure I put on myself to perform, to have answers, and to always be strong started eroding me from the inside. I still held the same beliefs, but my insides no longer matched my outsides. My actions and behaviors were, sometimes subtly and other times blatantly, in violation of my values. My figurative "check engine" light was flashing bright red, but I just kept on driving.

Back in London, following my big boardroom blowup, I nervously paced the streets and realized I'd lost my way. I'd accidentally become another shark in a suit. I allowed work to become a game of conquest and metrics, and it was slowly killing me. The mercenary in me had taken over, and my missionary heart was slowly dying—just as I had initially feared. I'd become the person I vowed I would never be.

In full transparency, things had gotten so bad that every four hours, I was swallowing a fistful of medications to temper my anxiety, help me sleep, and be a moderated version of myself. I drank too much, slept too little, and the heavy tension in my chest felt like a fifteen-pound plate of hot steel, making it hard to breathe. I started missing my kid's second-grade plays for one more client meeting. Reaching impossible quarterly revenue projections, sitting in endless, soul-corroding meetings, and eating dinner with strangers in fancy restaurants thousands of miles away from home ruled my life. It all culminated the day I was leaving for London. I was on my way out of the house. Things were not good in my marriage. My wife stood in our kitchen and told me as I walked out, "You know, it's easier when you're not here." God, she was right.

How did I get there?

It took me many months after that volatile London trip, but I peeled back the layers to discover the reasons behind my breakdown-breakthrough. Here is what I found:

- I stopped speaking up for what I believed.
- I started conforming to the lives and priorities of the people around me.
- I stopped doing work I loved and accepted a big salary, thinking big money would satisfy.
- I bought a big house, a country club membership, and we went on fancy vacations to medicate my incongruence.
- I restructured the definitions of success to match my life choices.

It's not that making money is a problem. And working hard isn't the problem. But when we start playing the game for money and lose sight of a deeper purpose and meaning, our missionary heart atrophies, and we lose all allegiance to our original mission. The twinkle in our eyes fades. Like Jerry—and like me—we can begin to hate our place in the world, if not ourselves.

It's All About Integration

Did you read the quote that began this chapter? As Mike Rowe, TV host of *Dirty Jobs,* says, "The mercenary posture will keep you profitable. The missionary position will keep you on top." What I think he's getting at is that it's not about being a mercenary *or* a missionary. The way out of this either/or tension is to integrate the mercenary and missionary by standing tall and unapologetically excelling in the mercenary world while operating out of a missionary heart. We can leverage the strengths of the mercenary by employing our competence, excellence, and vigor to achieve conquests and victories—but we can also keep our work anchored in our character, which maintains access to the fulfillment of the missionary.

To my mercenary friends—it may seem impossible to inhabit the mercenary world and bring your authentic self, but it's not. The way forward is to go back to the beginning and remember what you initially believed before money and success, pressure and power, and prestige and career ladders overran your story. Our workplaces are focused on delivering results, meeting the numbers, and sticking to the deadlines, all of which can make human connections feel like unwelcome distractions.

In the beginning, it might freak you out to think about how you could ever show up more authentically as an integrated human and bring your heart, body, mind, and soul to work. Here's my advice: Start small by getting to know the people you work with. Have lunch or take a break together, and run the risk of allowing them to know you.

My friend Chad is the newly appointed CFO at a global financial services company headquartered in Manhattan. He works in the epicenter of finance, where the captains of industry influence global markets. There isn't a lot of talk about heart and purpose. Chad has become a unicorn amid armies of mercenaries, embodying the spirit of a missionary, valuing financial results, and concurrently seeing past the balance sheets and earnings releases to invest in the people he's entrusted to lead.

After a recent acquisition, he flew to Denver to meet his newly acquired team. He shot me the following text: "There will be six of us at dinner. Looking to try a few new icebreakers to get the dialogue going. What table questions do you have for me without going too deep with them on their first time meeting their new boss?"

I suggested he ask each team member to introduce themselves by name and then close by answering the question, "What makes me unique?" I also told him, "You have to go first to model vulnerability and show them it's safe to be real with you." After dinner, he sent back this update: "One guy professionally races cars on the weekend. Another guy is training to be a boxer in a cancer charity event. So fun. Thanks, bud."

If Chad can lead with his missionary heart in his mercenary world, then so can we. What initially feels like risk results in a beautiful ROI (return on investment) and reward. Our missionary heart helps improve the quality of our human interactions, resulting in the creation of more trust and relational equity, and enables us to accomplish more together. In pure-blood mercenary environments that are void of trust, it's every man for himself, and our fears of self-preservation surface quickly. Our primal auto-response kicks into overdrive, and we spend most of our energy in a protective and reactive mind-set, which limits and hinders our progress.

Chad invited his new team to bring their whole selves to the significant challenges they will face together as they simultaneously face their responsibility to deliver predictable results. Imagine now when the going gets tough. Chad and his team members understand the strengths of their teammates; he knows he can rely on the gifts and abilities of a professional car racer and a boxer (who is fighting for a missionary cause—curing cancer) when the going gets tough.

When I look back on my own low moment—that business dinner in London that went sideways—I can see that everyone's mercenary was on overdrive. We were afraid of failing by missing our quarterly revenue commitments and disappointing ourselves and our investors. And we lacked the trust and relationship to work together collaboratively rather than competitively. The realities of profit and loss don't change when you integrate your missionary heart, but the nature of the interactions can take on a more creative, relational expression.

In the eye of the storm, our entire team was operating out of a reactive state. That's how Robert Anderson, founder of The Leadership Circle, defines it. After researching 155,000 leaders globally, The Leadership Circle programmatically translates its data-driven leadership assessment surveys onto a circular behavioral profile that's divided into four primary quadrants: Relationship, Reactive, Task, and Creative. Anderson's research quantifies our capacity to embody a "relational-task balance" of achieving while maintaining collaboration, caring connection, and purposeful vision.

Not long ago, I spent three days in Chicago training to become certified in The Leadership Circle profile assessment. As The Leadership Circle manual says, "We all know that great leadership is a complex mix of competency and inner states of being.... We start with the assumption that you are a marvelously complex and beautifully integrated whole person."[25] There is that phrase again—"integrated whole person"—reminding us that we can begin to interpret our behaviors, reactive tendencies, creative capabilities, and inner states as reflections of how well we are living from our missionary heart in this mercenary world.

If you're serious about discovering sustainable joy in your career, you're going to need both of these realities—mercenary and missionary—in your life. And no, this isn't simple—especially if you've been living in a hard-core mercenary culture. You won't do integrated wholeness perfectly and, at first, you might feel like you're the only one living and leading this way. But I'm here to tell you you're not alone. There are millions of people longing for wholeness in their work and personal lives, and there is a growing band of us willing to live and work in this integrated tension of mercenary and missionary. It is, I believe, the only way forward.

CHAPTER 7

WHAT'S WRONG?

What's Wrong with the World?
Dear Sirs, I am. Yours, G. K. Chesterton.

—Appeared in the *London Times*, 1910[26]

HI. MY NAME IS Aaron, and I'm a blamer. I realize that's not a confession you commonly hear. What's a blamer? When something goes wrong, the first thing a blamer wants to know is: "Whose fault is this?" That definition comes from Dr. Brené Brown, a research professor at the University of Houston. She has spent two decades studying courage, vulnerability, shame, and empathy. She has masterfully translated her research into best sellers like *Daring Greatly* and *Rising Strong*. Brown puts forth this proven yet simple definition when it comes to blame: "the discharging of discomfort and pain, and it has an inverse relationship with accountability."[27]

The zinger for me is, her research concludes that the reason we blame is "that it gives us some semblance of control."

I've got another confession. I've struggled with writing this chapter for months. I kept deleting it, revising it, and rewriting my outline in an attempt to justify why this topic is not essential to the overall arc of "firing your boss." If I'm honest, I think two things are driving my omission dreams. First, I don't want you to know about some of the ugliness in me. And second, I truly want to believe there are only three of you (us) who struggle with blame, so why dedicate a whole chapter to something that is irrelevant for 99.999 percent of readers? But with my hand on my heart, I cannot bring myself to spare you from this confrontation of moving away from blaming others to restoring the cornerstone of accountability. So here we go.

Please, feel free to skip this chapter if you are a shining example of character and never allow blame to distort your view of reality. That would mean:

a) You never project your frustration, anger, and disappointment onto others.
b) You never assign blame or fault to others that you later may regret and retract.
c) You consistently take 100 percent responsibility for your behaviors and decisions.

Go ahead, feel free.

I had a therapist once who said, "If you can spot it, you've got it." In other words, my ability to quickly recognize a less-than-desirable trait in others probably means I struggle with it myself.

Yeah, thanks a lot, therapist. But she was right. Unfortunately, as a recovering blamer, I can recognize a fellow blamer in seconds, and most don't even realize they are doing it.

Here's the Deal

Let me shoot you straight upfront. We blamers assign responsibility to everyone but ourselves, wholeheartedly believing we are justified. Plus, we are rarely accountable to ourselves or others for our decisions, our reactions, and our circumstances. We blamers may appear powerful in the moment, but under the surface we feel powerless.

In our careers, blamers always have a convincing story for why

- we didn't get that new job;
- we were fired or laid off;
- our customer wasn't happy;
- the project failed;
- we've worked at the same unsatisfying job for decades;
- our boss is ill equipped for his or her role;
- now isn't a good time for a change;
- our disappointments and frustrations are because of someone else's actions or decisions.

Now, pick one of those storylines that reflect a personal career disappointment or frustration. On a scale from one (lowest) to ten (highest) in terms of personal responsibility and ownership, give yourself a score based on this question: "How much responsibility did I have in that situation or relationship?" Sorry, but zero isn't an option for this exercise.

Maybe you were hoping the question I was going to ask was, "How much responsibility did the *other person* have in that situation or relationship?" Maybe you were hoping that so you could quickly and happily assign them a score of nine or ten, meaning, "They (the other party) were to blame for what happened." If so, let me welcome you to the club. You, like me, are a blamer. I know, I know. Thanks to Brené Brown, now we can't even enjoy the false satisfaction of projecting our discomfort onto others.

On some level it's fair. Allow me to share a few vulnerable upsets in my career. It hurt when I was told that my job was being eliminated the next month. It stung when I resigned, desiring to finish well, and instead of being given two weeks so I could leave with integrity, I was handed a box and told, "Get your shit and leave." Nine minutes later, I was driving away with a handful of belongings and unfinished goodbyes. It was difficult to hold my head high when my client humiliated me in front of his employees and my coworkers because he believed I held nitwit religious convictions causing me to give away all of my money to televangelists. Primal instincts almost took over when my trusted colleagues grew cold and protective when the new owners announce there were only four chairs available for the new executive team going forward, and there were five of us. I was the one left without a chair.

In those real-story moments, swimming with the sharks, the temptation is great to whip out and play the ace of spades blame card and reject any personal accountability for our contributions. But let me encourage you to resist that temptation. The upside of not playing the blame card allows for two very positive realities. First, it allows us to upgrade our clarity on any potential contribution and responsibilities we might have. My wife calls this "keeping her side of the street clean." Whatever mess we've made, we take the responsibility and clean it up. Second, resisting the temptation to blame allows us to apply laser precision to the fair portion of accountability attributable to the other person. We're not letting them off the hook, while at the same time agreeing that "it's not all their fault."

I have to tell you, this is the road less traveled. Very few people choose to walk the path toward accountability and away from blame. Turn on the nightly news, attend a school board meeting, log on your social media account, or listen in on family scuttlebutt. It's clear—blame is all the rage. The truth is, it always has been because it is easier than holding ourselves accountable for our own shit. I also have to tell you that, albeit difficult, eliminating the blame card from your hand frees you to experience other things, like contentment despite circumstances, and resilience grounded in a deep belief that we are here to do something meaningful with our life and work. Again, not easy, but so worth it.

Way back in 2011, I first wrote *Fire Your Boss* as a manifesto about leaving behind fear and finding career freedom. I think the best way to illustrate this big idea of ditching blame as the scapegoat and holding ourselves accountable is to rewind my career clock and share with you a snippet from that original version. I was in an extremely dysfunctional workplace, and I knew it. But everything changed the day my friend Jim and I took a walk in the parking lot outside our offices. In that conversation, he was the empathetic guide who helped me to retire using the blame card and to move forward with the empowerment that personal accountability brings.

My Blind Spot Became Clear

"I get it. I sign a contract and accept the terms of the agreement every time I cash a paycheck." Jim was right. It was an *aha!* moment for me.

At the time, I had a business dealing that accurately depicted this type of acceptance-through-actions contract. It was a contractual agreement between three parties that totaled seven figures. One of the parties never physically signed the deal, but they cashed the checks each year for their portion of the compensation. After a few years, the attorneys concluded that even though this party never signed the contract with pen and ink, they were acting according to the terms of the agreement and receiving compensation for doing so. Therefore, cashing the check was as good as signing the piece of paper.

And in my job, I was doing the same thing. By cashing my paycheck every two weeks, I was agreeing with the terms of my employment even though I wasn't externally condoning or accepting those terms. The conversation with Jim showed me I had some choices to make:

- I had to take ownership of my participation in the dysfunctional system.
- I could no longer blame or point fingers.

- I had to become a part of the solution.
- Or, I had to stop cashing my checks.

Accountability Sobriety

Each Monday morning that I returned to work after the previous week's workplace dysfunction, I taught the company that I was happy to be mistreated, undervalued, and underappreciated. Each week I'd say things like, "Well, I'm not sure I can be here if it stays like this." And every Monday I proved I was the world's worst bluffer by pointing my finger at everyone other than myself. When shenanigans took place that added to my frustration and disappointment, I dissected every conversation and created a running inventory list of blame.

The week would come to a close, I'd go home for the weekend, shake it off, then show up the next Monday morning ready to give it another try. In many ways, I was drinking from the bottle of blame, and I was drunk. It was a tough pill to swallow, but I finally realized that I was the only one to be held accountable for *my* frustrations and *my* emotions in that recurring drama (notice the emphasis on *my*). After I decided to get clean, so to speak, I made sure I was in a well-rested, creative, and empowered mind-set, and my conversation with my boss went something like this:

"I've realized that each Monday I return to work after (fill in the blank for the set of circumstances), I am the only one to blame. I'm teaching you how to treat me by permitting this kind of relationship. I apologize for showing you that I am okay with that kind of arrangement." Boom!

From that day forward, guess who became accountable and responsible for every conversation, every compensation negotiation, every reactionary behavior, and every decision I had to make?

Bingo. *Me*.

Even as I reread that snippet from nearly ten years ago, I feel how fresh this idea was to me. In terms of the hero's journey, I was way down under the surface in the depths of the unknown, facing my internal dragons and limiting beliefs, barely surviving my battle. But rising strong with this transformational insight was: "I have the power to choose and I'm accountable for me." Over time, my accountability sobriety evolved to include: "I'm accountable for my emotions of frustration and disappointment. No one can make me feel a certain way. I have agency over my emotions. I'm accountable for my actions and responses. I alone retain the responsibility for my behaviors and my reactions. I am not a helpless victim, and no one is forcing me to work here. I am responsible for how I teach others to treat and respect me." Boom!

At the turn of the nineteenth century, the *London Times* posed a provocative editorial question asking readers to respond to this sentence: "What's wrong with the world?" Can you imagine the *New York Times* or the *Washington Post* inviting answers to this question today? I think we could accurately predict a volcano of scathing projections of blame and pain erupting from readers. I suspect that the world was an imperfect place in 1910, and everyday citizens were as prone to deflect personal responsibility as we are today. To the *Times*' surprise, English philosopher, theologian, and journalist G. K. Chesterton penned this vulnerable admonition of responsibility to their question:

Dear Sirs, I am.

Let that settle in, friends. Give Chesterton's antidote to blame a moment to rest in your heart. Then apply it to your career upsets. His two-word answer serves as a hair-of-the-dog for our more courageous path of accountability leading us toward freedom and transformative change.

An important distinction to call out is that by choosing accountability, we are not exonerating others of their responsibility. In my story, a part of the truth was that my boss was a challenging human to interact with regularly. Blame backfired on me as I allowed myself to become enmeshed in the drama of my boss's decisions and behaviors, and I became stuck in a downward spiral of powerlessness. To create the future I desired, I had to hold others responsible for their actions while decoupling my responses, my decisions, my dreams, and my hopes. It was, and is, difficult. But it is incredibly empowering. Now you may not be ready to leap to G. K.'s conclusion, and that's okay. I'm confident that he too found himself on a journey of challenging his interpretations from the viewpoint of taking a personal inventory of his contributing missteps, shortcomings, and character defects.

Here's a personal insight that fissured up about myself from the viewpoint of my boss and company. Around this same period of awakening, my friend Morgan and I were on a bike ride together early one Saturday morning in the crisp Colorado springtime. As we pounded out the surrounding hills, I shared my realization with him. He'd listened to me bitching and moaning for years about how my boss did this or didn't do that. My stories blurred together and became indistinguishable, except this time I had something new to say: "Can you imagine what it must be like for my boss to manage me? I bet I'm giving her the biggest rash." It was exterior evidence that I'd come to internalize Chesterton's gospel of "I am" and adopted the perspective of my boss with a genuine spirit of compassion and curiosity. "What must it be like to manage me?" It is a courageous question, and it yielded a more balanced view of my predicaments.

The upside of holding myself accountable enabled me to see my shortcomings and put myself in the shoes of my boss, employees, and clients. Here are a few specifics I humbly realized:

- I can be very impatient and irritable when a process needs to be followed which I perceive impedes progress.
- At times, I think rules apply to everyone else but me.
- I falsely assume everyone understands what to do and why we are doing it. I don't take the time to explain my thinking fully.

Do you remember when I said I didn't want to write this chapter because it would reveal some of my own ugliness? Well, there ya go. I'd spent so many years blaming other people and situations that I'd become blind to my contribution to the challenges. A friend of mine twelve years in recovery says, "If you want to get out of the hole you're in, you first have to put down the shovel." After decades of developing my craft as a blamer, I surrendered my shovel and stopped digging. Robert Anderson, that thirty-year visionary in the field of leadership development, says, "We can take responsibility for what is going on around us and within us rather than blaming others (especially bosses) and circumstances for why current reality does not match what we want."[28]

Change What You Can

Friends, whatever workplace grievances you have, your disappointments, and the losses you've experienced, they are all true. If we'd been witnesses with you, I'm confident we'd empathize with you. Period. And, I also know that, like with my stories, there is a more empowering way forward, starting with admitting—even if only to yourself at first—that you too have shoveled out a few clumps of dirt and added to the depth of the hole you're in. Once we begin owning new measures of accountability, we can shift our energy away from the problem or crisis toward new, creative ways of engaging, like identifying what you can productively influence.

At the moment, I'm on a plane to New Orleans. The pilot told us that today is the anniversary of Nelson Mandela's release from his twenty-seven-year incarceration for opposing apartheid—legally enforced segregation in South Africa. After his release, he became the first black president of South Africa and led his people by creating the Truth and Reconciliation Commission. Victims and persecutors alike took the stand, broadcast on public television, and retold their stories of hate and violence, concluding with a blanket promise of forgiveness in the form of a pardon for all perpetrators who gave their testimony. Think with me for a moment. What if blame—"the discharging of discomfort and pain"—would have taken center stage in Nelson Mandela's life and leadership? Where would South Africa be today? In his own words,

"As I walked out the door toward the gate that would lead to my freedom, I knew if I didn't leave my bitterness and hatred behind, I'd still be in prison."[29]

I imagine us together at a live McKinsey & Company leadership workshop, and as I scan the room measuring the resonance of this message, your eyes are telling me a lot. You want to know what to do next, how to operationalize the accountability and empowerment available to you. Let's start with a practice of noticing when you find yourself reaching for the blame card. Here's a mantra that you can repeat in the moment setting you up for a new more creative response.

I bet you've heard this before, but you may not know its origin. Alcoholics Anonymous has adopted theologian-philosopher Reinhold Niebuhr's "Serenity Prayer":

> *God grant me the serenity to accept the things I*
> *cannot change, courage to change the things I can,*
> *and wisdom to know the difference.*[30]

Throughout our careers we will face many challenges, suffer disappointments, and possibly weather long seasons of difficulty. "Firing your boss" is about becoming the kind of person who is accountable for your workplace happiness, engagement, and contentment. We forgive those who wrong us while holding them responsible for their actions. And when we are tempted to blame others for our circumstances and current realities, we resist, choose to take the higher road of personal responsibility, and change what we can.

CHAPTER 8

THOSE DAMN FENCES

NO FISHING. SERIOUSLY, THAT'S what it reads, in black capital letters on a bright yellow background. The neighborhood association recently put up the sign near the trail that leads to the pond not far from my house. At first it drove me crazy. I couldn't believe the HOA was attempting to restrict me from fishing in my backyard. But then I remembered something about myself—I've always hopped fences. I guess my curiosity and spirit of adventure are stronger than my fear of getting caught on the wrong side of the fence.

Back Then

Back in college, inspired by the movie *Stand by Me*, I convinced my roommates to walk the nearby train tracks for an overnight adventure. We weren't searching for a dead body, just a little Texas springtime fresh air. Equipped with little more than our gypsy-sized backpacks and a bit of wanderlust, we started out, hugging the tracks east along the Brazos River. Along that central Texas route, there were miles and miles of private fence line posted at regular intervals with warning signs like "No Trespassing—Will Prosecute." These fences and signs had all been put in place by the lords and barons of those wild places—Texas ranchers. By the time dusk fell, our hobo curiosities had been satisfied. So we left the tracks and hopped a fence (without a visible sign) to set up our tent. The tent was glowing from the dull-flamed candle lantern, and I faintly recall someone reading aloud Jack London's Yukon stories.

Before dawn, we woke to the blind sounds of a screeching truck and cussing. Mr. Texas Rancher was having none of our explorer's spirit. He was *pissed*. He wanted to know what the hell possessed us to hop his fence, set up a tent, and trespass in his field. Little did we know we'd blindly ransacked the home of a thousand-pound bull with Texas-size horns. Mr. Texas Rancher's fence was there to protect everyone from his beast. After a red-faced lecture, he let us go, each of us promising never to be so stupid ever again.

And Now

Back to the warning sign in my backyard. My neighborhood is named The Farm. It's a dwindling outpost of a wilder Colorado amid suburbia. In the 1940s, the original owners—a cowboy family—ran horses and cattle here. They also named each of the five ponds on their property after their daughters. The newly designated off-limits pond is called Jenny's Lake. Although a few barbed-wire fence remnants remain, most of what is there is newly erected, split-rail fences neatly framing manicured lawns.

At the time of our move-in, we and our four other pioneering neighbors were surrounded by these combined fence lines. To me, they were more like story props than protection from anything wild. Without hesitation, I jumped every fence I could find to explore the trails, ponds, and wide-open spaces of our new place. At neighborhood BBQs, I learned that my rule-following neighbors had yet to cross any fence lines. They all stayed inside the boundaries set up some eighty years ago. For the life of me, I could not understand this, although my gut tells me it has something to do with "safety."

On the wild side of things, beyond the fence lines, I caught a five-pound largemouth bass on my fly rod and discovered an abandoned rowboat that we have since refurbished and dubbed the SS *Joy Boat*. Sometimes at lunch, I'd walk down between conference calls with my fly rod in hand and reel in ten to fifteen fish. For two years, I never saw another person. One night after dusk, I hopped my back fence and meandered just out of sight and tucked into the base of the hundred-year-old Ponderosa pine trees and camped under the Colorado sky. Another night, my friend Alex and I brought our wives down for a double date on the floating dock and toasted the fading purple mountain sunset. I could go on.

Here's the kicker: In the beginning, none of the now-common "No Trespassing" signs were posted. There was just old fence. But this summer, everything changed. The barricades came down and fleets of bulldozers and earthmovers arrived. Now the developer is on the warpath to clear the way for five hundred new homes. Every fence, shrub, and homestead relic is being devoured. I find it interesting that suddenly my neighbors have become incredibly curious. Everyone is exploring the wild side. Word is spreading fast about the great fishing and walking trails. I ran into a guy the other day who told me he discovered Jenny's Lake listed on a local fishing app.

The irony to me is that no one even seemed remotely curious when the fences were up. I assume they believed it wasn't safe to trespass. Also, though there were no signs and no warnings, everyone stayed inside the established boundaries. The minute they came down, everyone's perceptions changed. Now, "it must be safe." Mr. Colorado Developer got word that anarchy is ensuing, like Mr. Fishing App wandering in to take home prize-winning bass. That's what's behind the new signs boldly outlawing my favorite pastimes, starting with *No Fishing*. Now I'm waiting for more signs to suddenly appear: *No Running, No Camping*, and *No Drinking*.

Just Beyond the Façade

We humans tend to stay inside the boundary lines and don't ask a lot of questions about what's beyond the borders. Maybe we have moments of curiosity, but we quickly talk ourselves out of our adventurous dreams and fall back into our repeatable play-it-safe mode. Can you endure another movie reference? Great, thanks. Ever watched the movie *The Truman Show* with Jim Carrey? The main character, Truman Burbank, finds himself growing increasingly curious about the border lines of his life. He lives in this perfect little Cape Cod Eastern Seashore town—a cross between

Andy Griffith's Mayberry and George Bailey's Bedford Falls. As idyllic as it is, he increasingly cannot contain his curiosity about faraway lands and a beautiful woman he'd once encountered. For three decades, he followed all the societal rules, was well behaved, and was an outstanding citizen.

But then a moment arrives when Truman learns that everything in his world is part of an elaborately orchestrated TV show in which he is the main and only character not in on the joke. Born inside the TV show, raised and reared to accept his reality, Truman was happy and content, until he finally wasn't. The movie culminates with Truman finding his freedom by hopping fences and exploring the wild side. In his case, his fence-hopping started with navigating a sailboat across an imaginary ocean that abruptly ended as the bow gouged a hole in the fake painted backdrop of a blue sky. Freedom wasn't as far away as he feared. It was just beyond the façade.

Our careers are full of fences and signs with big black letters claiming imminent danger and consequences for breaking the rules or going outside the boundary of safety. We've been convinced that if we follow the rules, we will be rewarded with the safety, security, predictability, and financial comfort we desire. Here are a few of the spoken and unspoken but advertised benefits and implied warnings for those of us who stay on the safe side of the career fence lines. The enduring fable of playing it safe and following the rules. The never-ending promise that if you do this, you'll be healthy, wealthy, and wise.

Here are the rules we're told to follow and the rewards we can expect if we color inside the lines:

Go get a good-paying job and hold onto it for dear life. Good jobs are few and far between, so be thankful if you're one of the few. Work hard and rest very little; two weeks a year is plenty to recharge your batteries. Don't cause any scenes. Put your head down and grind it out. When you're young, it's important to make as much money as you can so that you can enjoy your retirement later. There will be plenty of time then to rest and play and enjoy your life. Remember, very few people love what they do for a living.

Pick something you're good at, develop your skills, and then spend the rest of your life doing that. You'll get paid more for expertise, and if you don't love it anymore, well, tough shit. Being a grown-up is about responsibility, and fun is a luxury that few experience. Buy as big a house as the bank will allow. Go on fancy vacations (during those two weeks) and buy lots of stuff, for these are your rewards for working so hard. Save money in your 401(k), and you will retire at age sixty-five as a millionaire and travel the world while eating caviar. You're going to be rich, so keep that as your North Star.

I know these warnings and promises aren't written down anywhere, and they are both mildly accurate and distortions of the truth when taken too far. In my mind's eye though, I see these false warning signs all along invisible fences intended to hem us into our own personal version of *The Truman Show*. Having a good-paying job is terrific, with the footnote of also enjoying your work. But beware of the implicit warning that's always there—if you leave your good-paying job, think of the heartache, uncertainty, and public humiliation you will face if you hop the fence and explore the unknown places. You might end up living back in your parent's basement with your spouse and four kids. These warnings are what author Rob Bell calls "vague, ominous rumblings,"[31]—unclear repercussions and consequences that linger beyond the fence line.

Care of the Soul

I have a friend who has worked for the same company since college. He's currently holding out for his thirtieth anniversary. He puts on a good show, is always chipper, and never complains about work—or much of anything, come to think of it. I just learned the real story from his family: he's miserable. He's afraid to jump the fence, not because he is a rule follower at heart, but because he perceives the risk of venturing into the unknown as a scarier proposition than the discomfort of being miserable until retirement. In other words, he's scared.

Okay, time out, friends. This is not simply my friend's story. It's *our* story. Regardless of whether we have a pension, or stock options, or a pending promotion, or simply a safe-and-predictable-Monday-through-Friday-easy-money gig, we stay inside the boundary lines and do the expected thing for decades at a time, all the while forgetting to ask the more important question: *What is this costing me?* What soul-cost are we paying one rounding zero at a time?

I'm sure in my friend's case, he has a nice pension from thirty years of staying inside the boundaries of safety and predictability, white-knuckling his way to the finish line. I'm also sure that once he's put to pasture, he will find ways to live safely inside the fence line of retirement. But is that the only option? Some straight-and-narrow that's ultimately just narrow? Is there not another option?

A way to navigate the complexity of providing for our families while doing work we love and living with an explorer's spirit?

Bronnie Ware is a palliative care provider and also a best-selling author. Her book *The Top Five Regrets of the Dying* captured her results over years of sharing the last weeks and days with her patients who'd moved home from the hospital to die. In their final conversations together, the patients discussed any regrets they had or anything they wished they would have done differently. Here's what she heard. Take a good listen, keeping in mind this idea of staying on the safe side of the fence or hopping the fence and exploring the unknown.

The top five:

1. I wish I'd dared to live a life true to myself, not the life others expected of me.
2. I wish I hadn't worked so hard.
3. I wish I'd dared to express my feelings.
4. I wish I had stayed in touch with my friends.
5. I wish that I had let myself be happier.[32]

From where I'm standing, these end-of-life wishes are not warning signs as much as they are invitations. Not all fences are keeping us safe. Some are advertising safety but are actually preventing us from experiencing more fulfillment and satisfaction in our careers. I view Bronnie Ware's findings as field notes from those at the end of their life—veterans of life looking back with earnest clarity and saying, "I wish I would have explored more of the wild places, hopped fences, risked more in relationships and how I spent my time. I wish I'd not adhered to all of the unwritten and unspoken rules of society, and I wish I'd given myself permission to deviate from the narrow script of success."

Here's my advice. I'm not able to provide you directives on which fences you should hop and which ones pose a real danger. Only you can do that. I can promise you that some barriers are story props and relics. "Firing your boss" is about developing the skill to identify those fences that are protecting you from real danger—like a thousand-pound Texas bull. And although this sounds almost silly, I've found the best place to start is by asking, "Is this fence real?" Let me give you a personal example.

A few years ago, when I decided to leave my software career behind, hop the fence, and go explore a new career as a consultant for culture transformations, I was genuinely nervous. If I stayed the course in the software field, I was guaranteed $200,000 a year, an executive position, stock options, and lots of responsibility yielding predictability and the perception of safety. By hopping the fence and leaving behind those guarantees, I explored Bronnie Ware's antidote to regret. I let myself be happier and dared to live a life true to myself. Full disclosure? It required me to bottom out our savings account, pray a lot, and travel to Europe for training. (Did I mention I pray a lot?) It was scary at moments, full of uncertainty, and simultaneously exhilarating. And just what did I find on the other side of the fence? A new career with McKinsey & Company working alongside some of the most talented people on the planet inside the globe's most successful companies. There were real risks, no doubt, but none of them could sink my story. The best part is that all of the benefits and rewards are a thousand times more rewarding, and my future is so much brighter.

The Way I See Things

I'm betting many of you identify with my friend who is eight years from retirement. I can imagine that must be excruciatingly difficult to grapple with—the guarantee of financial certainty by staying your current course partnered with the fixed return of slow soul corrosion. I'm not like Bronnie Ware's patients, at the end of their earthly lives. But I was at the end of a very literal way of living that, oddly enough, felt like I was dying on the inside. So I hopped the fence. And although difficult, I would rather hold firm to the guaranteed adventure of personal growth and an increase in wealth by living a life with fewer regrets.

Here are the career guiding principles that I discovered along the path of daring to live a life true to myself.

Do work that you passionately believe in.

As Steve Jobs reminds us in chapter 1 ("The Big Idea"): "Don't settle." Through the course of my career, I've consistently recalibrated based on ebbs and flows in my passion and engagement levels. I've learned that my curiosity has driven most of my career shifts and adjustments. When I start feeling bored and uninterested, I know that my passion and engagement will begin to wane. My passion level is like a dashboard light, and when it starts turning yellow or red, I start asking myself questions about whether this is a temporary blip or if something bigger is going on inside me.

Work for a company you believe in.

If you work for a physician, you should probably like caring for people. If you work for an accounting firm, you need to believe in the value of the work you do for your clients. Every company has a personality and an impact, no matter how big or small, that it makes on the world. I worked in advertising for a decade before I started my career in software. One reason I made a change was that I began to realize that my job was to convince people to buy products and services they often didn't need. My passion dashboard light started flashing yellow, and I became conscious of dissonance within me. I no longer believed in the purpose behind the work I did every day.

Work with people you enjoy.

We often spend more time at work than with our own families. Just like with a winning team, it's essential to enjoy the people you work with. You don't have to be best friends, nor do you have to love everyone. But it sure makes our career experience a lot more fulfilling when we share a sense of harmony and positivity contributed to by our colleagues.

Save money every month, but don't count on your 401(k) to be enough by itself to send you into early retirement as millionaires.

Our modern world is fascinated with wealth and its acquisition. Today, peppered throughout the US population of nearly

330 million people, there are a reported 11 million millionaires (roughly 3 percent of the population).[33] Statistically speaking, most of us won't become millionaires and retire early, despite the promises of the headlines. The liberating news is that we can invest our energy in finding and doing work we love while saving a portion of our earnings every month. Whether you amass a million dollars or create a little nest egg, the best part is that happy people who love their work tend to make more money.[34]

Pursue your dreams and adventures now. Don't wait.

Every three months, schedule some adventure on your calendar. We aren't guaranteed a certain number of days on this earth. Thinking back to Bronnie Ware's end-of-life regrets, I am not willing to wait until "someday" to enjoy my life and pursue my dreams. I have a college friend who asks me the same question about every ten years: "How do you play so much?" He asked me that question last summer after I finished a hundred-mile backpacking trip through the Wind River mountain range in Wyoming. My answer is always the same: "I choose to." Our calendar and our checkbook don't lie, and the best way to make your dreams happen is to schedule them and *go big*!

Take healthy risks.

Taking risk inherently means that it might not work. The plan may fail, the idea might flop, and the new venture may never get traction. But the question is which is worse—to try and fail, or to live with the regret? I met a guy once at a children's birthday party, and he shared with me that he'd just left his high-tech day job to become a professional clown. That's right—a clown. His poor wife was standing next to him staring at the ground, attempting to muster social support for her man. I didn't have to listen long to understand that the risk he was running was not healthy (and not very funny). He was ejecting from a career to pursue a dream that was actually sort of a hobby. In other words, he didn't have a well-founded plan. This one is a "both-and"—you can take healthy risks and maintain some semblance of a plan.

Become the kind of person you are proud to be.

Dr. Richard Ryan and Dr. Tim Kasser of the University of Rochester conducted a 1996 study surveying one hundred adults about their life aspirations and personal values. Their results were then mapped against standard measurements of psychological well-being. Those participants who adhered to goals "tied to others' approval, like fame, reported significantly higher levels of distress than those interested primarily in self-acceptance and friendship."[35] When we focus on becoming a person that we are proud of, no one can take that away from us.

Choose happiness.

Leith put up a small four-by-four-inch pinup card on the wall of our guest bathroom inviting all who enter to "Choose Happiness." I love that. How often are you purposely pivoting your emotional mind-set to the intentional gear of happiness? Our outlook is a predictor of the outcome. Sitting just below happiness is the engine of joy. Develop the purposeful discipline of refilling your joy tank with small deposits every day. When I'm feeling down, I often go for a quick ten-minute walk around the block. The poet Wallace Stevens wrote, "Perhaps / The truth depends on a walk around the lake." I agree.

Don't wait until your retirement years. Enjoy your life today, take lots of time off work to rest and play. Invest in relationships with your family and friends.

I subscribe to a principle I first read in *The 4-Hour Workweek* by Tim Ferriss. He prescribes taking what he calls mini-rests and mini-retirements. Instead of waiting until our retirement years to take time off, we can start introducing intentional breaks along the way. A few years ago, I started taking two to four months off every two and a half years. At first, it felt delusional to throw out the idea that somehow the stars would align so that I could step away from work. But I'm living proof that it can happen if you choose to make it happen. My friend Rachael O'Meara wrote an excellent book on the topic, *Pause: Harnessing the Life-Changing Power of Giving Yourself a Break*. Rachael lays out the case for why you deserve a break and how to practically step away for restoration, recalibration, and reconnection with the people you love.

Measure wealth by your experiences. Not by the stuff you buy.

Four years ago, our family sold or gave away nearly everything we owned. After a decade, our five-bedroom suburban home had become bloated and full of stuff we no longer knew we had or needed. I mean, who needs seven pocketknives anyway? Systematically, a story deserving of its own book, we decluttered and simplified our life's belongings down to a few things. Our modern world is on a treadmill of consumption, and most of the things we have we don't need (notice the success of Marie Kondo). I've discovered the wealth of things you cannot buy and now measure value by the connections we create with the people we love. Me, my daughter, my brother, and my nephews just returned from a 2,200-mile road trip in our 1974 VW Bus through the desert Southwest. We slept in the Route 66 Wigwam Motel, visited the Grand Canyon in a snowstorm, and gazed on the Monument Valley Navajo Tribal Park while cooking up a pot of ramen noodles. Those memories won't end up in a Goodwill donation box. Not a chance.

"Firing your boss" is about stepping into open spaces, hopping the fences that are hemming you in, and learning to look beyond the warning signs to chart your course away from regret and toward a life you are proud to live, a person you're proud to be, and pursuing work you believe in. There is a money-back guarantee that you will stare at yourself in the mirror and smile, knowing you took the chance. You'll lay your head down at night with the satisfaction that your young guide is proud of you for pushing past the fear of failure. The grand prize is that you will have truly mesmerizing stories to tell your grandchildren about the fences you hopped and what wonders you found just on the other side.

CHAPTER 9

LIVED AND UNLIVED LIVES

How much did they first pay you to give up
on your dreams?
Twenty-seven grand a year.
And when were you going to stop and come back
and do what makes you happy?
Good question.
You have an opportunity here, Bob. This is a rebirth.
If not for you, do it for your children.

—*Up in the Air*[36]

A **PRETTY FORCEFUL EXCHANGE,** isn't it? George Clooney's character is terminating a bewildered man in his mid-fifties who, decades before, accepted his first job at this company for an annual salary of $27,000 and subsequently gave up on his dream of becoming a chef. After culinary college, when faced with the pressures of life, he chose the fork in the road heading toward predictability.

Now fast-forward a few decades and add a mortgage payment, a kid with chronic illness, a bad case of "my life sucks," and now he's earning $100,000 a year running a call center, all while stuck on the treadmill of life. Christmases came and went, birthdays and anniversaries had been celebrated, kids' soccer games had been won and lost, mergers were weathered, and now, downsized, he nobly acquiesced his way to this career upset. We aren't privy to where his story goes next. What we do know is that his choices aren't simple. This isn't a book about quitting your job on a whim to chase your fantasies to become a world-class chef. We're dealing with a complex symbiosis where we live in reality, foster our desires, maintain our responsibilities, and care for our soul—none of which is simple.

The Middle-Aged Man and the Sea

When I was in middle school, the father of one of my friends had this intoxicating coffee table book with exquisite pictures of sailing adventures. In fragments, he confided in me about the call the sea had on his soul. By day, his calloused hands serviced commercial heating and air-conditioning units for his clients. He was the kind of man whose word was his bond, and some of those words persuaded one of his customers to give me my first job flipping hamburgers. He also, on occasion, took my little brother and me rock climbing, where I witnessed him in action working the climbing rope like a jib sail.

We'd return to my friend's family room where his father would spin vinyl albums like Dylan's *Blood on the Tracks* or Crosby, Stills & Nash, and profess, "I'm taking the whole family, and we're sailing around the world." I could hear the inflection in his voice increase and brighten when personifying the command of his future thirty-foot craft. I admired him for his spirit of adventure and the unabashed freedom he embodied while vulnerably sharing his daydreams of sunburns, seagulls, and untethered living. I would have gladly followed him as a stowaway. His do-it-yourself family was primed for it. His wife was a gritty non-conformist ultra-athlete, and his kids were farm-hearty and already kin to isolation. They would be the perfect deck crew for the maiden voyage on the USS *Wanderlust*.

I'm disappointed to report that my friend's father never bought a sailboat and, to my knowledge, their family never even rented one for an afternoon. Unfortunately, the vessel of their life shipwrecked against the jagged rocks of middle age, divorce, and the unrest I imagine resulted from refusing one too many times the call of the sea. Duty called, as it understandably does for us all. And like most of us, he answered. What aches my heart the most is how the overwhelming volume of responsibility subdues the steady transponder pulse of desire. But even if our hearts grow deaf to its beat, I believe desire stays alive. It's in our bones.

I genuinely understand why our ambitions of sailing around the world or becoming a chef get shelved and downgraded to priority zero. Our once clear aspirations become bashful fantasies placed right next to the trophies from high school, the dusty coffee table books, and the empty photo albums from the trips and adventures never taken. It happened to me, too.

I mentioned earlier the actor Jim Carrey. His dad was a fantastic professional jazz saxophone player in a swing band. A moment arrived which presented him the opportunity to move to the United States and following his music-making visions. Like any good father, the burden of his family responsibilities weighed heavy on him. So he chose to put his saxophone on the shelf in favor of a more predictable income stream. Carrey's dad settled down to become an accountant. "And as time wore on, it wore him down, and he got a little bit bitter, especially when he lost his job when he was fifty-one." Carrey chokes back tears giving us the gut-punch life lesson: "When you compromise and you fail, it really hurts. It hurts even more than failing at what you love."[37]

We can't guarantee success in our careers or our lives. At every step of the way, we run the risk of fumbling, stumbling, and failing. The double whammy is when we fail at a vocation that we don't love, which then has a way of contributing to our inability to be happy at home. Jim Carrey took the polar-opposite approach, propelling him into an all-or-nothing career of comedy. "You can fail at what you don't want, so you might as well take a chance on doing what you love. There's really no choice to be made."[38]

I wish it were as easy as saying, "Go play your saxophone!" or "Go sail the globe!" or "Go become a chef instead of a call-center manager." But I recognize it is not. Most things in our lives worth doing are hard. They involve honest struggle. Staying clear of a magic answer or guaranteed prescription, I have a few stories for you that illustrate real people walking the path of pursuing their dreams while balancing their commitments and responsibilities.

Lived and Unlived Lives

Last weekend my wife and I listened to a local garage band play at the neighborhood brewhouse. The ringleader wore wannabe-rock-star white tennis shoes with rainbow brushstrokes and a free-living tie-dyed T-shirt. He bounced like an unmedicated ADD adolescent and sang like a slightly buzzed Tom Petty. If I didn't know better, I'd mistake him as a professional Peter Pan—a boy with no interest in ever growing up. But I do know better. The truth is, by day he's a successful eye surgeon. My sister-in-law heard him deliver a keynote continuing-education address at a recent ophthalmologist conference. Every Friday he closes his clinic, and for that one day he flips personas from blue-scrubs surgeon to garage-band rock star. On the eve of turning fifty years old, with four kids, a wife, and a distinguished medical career, he's threading the needle between commitments and life passions. Fortunately, he's proof that there are unconventional ways to negotiate trade-offs within our realities while not compromising on the pursuit of our dreams and soul's thirsts.

Steven Pressfield is a best-selling author, creative, and master yogi when it comes to issuing woes to those of us who attempt to avoid the fire in our bellies, sell out, and numb our soul's calling. He cuts to the chase in his book *The War of Art* and names our enemy:

> Most of us have two lives. The life we live, and the unlived life within us. Between the two stands Resistance. Have you ever brought home a treadmill and let it gather dust in the attic? Ever quit a diet, a course of yoga, a meditation

practice? ... Are you a writer who doesn't write, a painter who doesn't paint, an entrepreneur who never starts a venture? Then you know what Resistance is....

Have you heard this story? Woman learns she has cancer, six months to live. Within days she quits her job, resumes the dream of writing Tex-Mex songs she gave up to raise a family (or starts studying classical Greek, or moves to the inner city and devotes herself to tending babies with AIDS). Woman's friends think she's crazy; she herself has never been happier. There's a postscript. Woman's cancer goes into remission.

Is that what it takes? Do we have to stare death in the face to make us stand up and confront Resistance?[39]

Standing up and owning our reverberating pulses of passion rarely comes down to a singular event or momentary intersection with destiny. There is a daily-ness to our noble and sensible resignations. We dutifully go about our lives for years, decades even, and suddenly we look up to find ourselves with parts or whole swatches of our lives unlived.

Dualistic Thinking

We strong-arm ourselves to select one of two supposedly mutually exclusive paths, maintaining a mental model of opposites.

It's what author and Franciscan friar Richard Rohr refers to as "dualistic thinking":

> The dualistic mind is essentially binary, either/or thinking. It knows by comparison, opposition, and differentiation. It uses descriptive words like good/evil, pretty/ugly, smart/stupid, not realizing there may be a hundred degrees between the two ends of each spectrum. Dualistic thinking works well for the sake of simplification and conversation, but not for the sake of truth or the immense subtlety of actual personal experience.[40]

STAY THE COURSE	OR	PURSUE MY DREAMS
+Care for my family	or	−Risk Failure
+Guarantee safety and comfort	or	−Become destitute

But for most of us, things are rarely that black and white. In reality, our choices are more subtle, more both-and, like our eye-doctor friend, who I think is heroic, by the way. "Do I not see patients on Fridays and give up the thousand bucks a week so that I can spend an entire day pursuing my love of music which only makes me two hundred dollars a month playing bar gigs?" His answer? "Yes!" And does that set in motion a tension? Another resounding "Yes!"

Sometimes there is debris blocking the flow of our dreams in our belly to taking action. I paid a therapist $150 an hour to help me surface my compromising, self-sabotaging reasons for maintaining my "Unlived Life." Here they are in rank and order of power and prevention:

1. My work responsibilities
2. My family's needs
3. Shit I gotta do
4. Fear of my future

If you're picturing me reclined on a velour couch while my therapist is writing down my responses, no, this wasn't that kind of therapy. It was more like a drama class than a clinical session. As we verbally worked our way under the waterline of my iceberg, what began to surface were these partners in my compromising behaviors. It sounded something like this:

"What's the problem, Aaron?"

"I'm not living the life I want to live."

"Explain what you mean."

"I want to write a book, but I'm not. I want to go on a big adventure with my brother, but I won't pull the trigger."

"Okay, and what stands in your way of doing these things that are important to you?"

As her questions continued, she coached me through a process of arranging her office items as props in my complicit story and attaching roles to each physical object representing one of the preventative forces that contribute to my paralysis. If you're totally freaked out and so grateful you didn't have to do this, I get it. Just stay with me here, this is good.

Here are the items and what they symbolized: Her office chair (work), green plant (family), wastebasket (shit I gotta do), and a calculator (fear of my future), which was perfect for calculating how behind I felt. Each item was arranged according to its priority of authoritative veto power. Taking in the reality of my life-sculpture, and with tears in my eyes, I arranged myself at the back of the line, realizing for the first time why I regularly compromise what I want. It was an awakening—"I'm at the back of the line, and they outnumber me. I lose every time."

My false unconscious beliefs became clear. Only when all of my work responsibilities are accomplished, my family's needs are met, and the shit I gotta do is taken care of can I consider doing things for myself. I was living truly at the back of the line. I'd become a professional at deferring the life I want to live. Those adventure trips I'd read about in *National Geographic*? And sea-kayaking in Scotland while sampling whiskey from every port-city distillery we'd pass? Those all stayed unlived, and it was killing me.

> *You think Resistance isn't real?*
> *Resistance will bury you.*
> —Steven Pressfield[41]

As if running the gauntlet of work, family, and shit I gotta do weren't tricky enough, if I successfully navigated the first three obstacles demanding dutiful production of results, the wild card "fear of my future" would surface, shaming me into play-it-safe submission. "Yes, you're right, that three thousand dollars for a trip to Scotland would be put to better use in my 401(k)."

With my therapist's direction, I walked to the front of the line and witnessed my operating reality prohibiting my ability to act upon my desires. I needed a new heart-centric operating system.

So I graciously and firmly informed my then-current operating system: "Thanks for helping me get to where I am today. You guys have served me well. You've also given me some terrible advice, and I'm tired of you winning all of the time. I am taking back the lead, and *I* am running my life going forward."

Up until that point, I'd spent the last number of years making sure everyone and everything was taken care of while quietly neglecting myself. It's fine to make sure everyone at the party is having a good time, just as long as you are, too. This transformational experience illuminated my mental and emotional negotiations so that with new awareness I could begin making different choices. I was ready to start having a good time again.

Finding Rhythm

So what does this mean for you? Do you need to find a local therapist to create an office-furniture sculpture of your interior dream-squelching frictions? I will leave that decision to you. My point, though, is that below our waterline, in our hidden depths, there are valid reasons for our chosen behaviors and choices—the why we do what we do and don't do. The opportunity for us is to build awareness and distinguish the fears and anxieties that prevent us from living full lives. By the way, just so you know, I took the sea-kayaking trip, and the Scottish whiskey tasted terrific after a long day of navigating Loch Etive. I paddled up to castles and chased seals. I highly recommend it. To say it's been life-saving is an understatement.

I want to round out this chapter with encouragement for you. And the best way I've found to do that is via stories. Here are a handful of other people giving the big swollen middle finger to compromise and finding ways to negotiate life-giving trade-offs. They've found the rhythm, and I love watching them dance.

I recently ran into a former coworker who by day is a marketing consultant. But at night, for the last thirteen years, he chipped away steadily at a writing project. Now he's got a literary agent and is shopping the fiction manuscript he wrote. My next-door neighbor Walt is a physician by day. But at night, over the last eleven years, has assembled personal accounts, radio communications, and old hand-written love letters from his father to his mom. He's made field trips to libraries and battlegrounds to piece together a true World War II story about the famous Lipizzaner horses and the heroes not to be forgotten (especially his dad). I feel confident you will see this story on the big screen one day.

These two guys are singing their song while they live and negotiate trade-offs with their time, attention, and resources. They're living true lives. They've found the rhythm.

That's just two stories. The amazing thing is, I've got more—stories of individuals and families who've pushed the pause button on the treadmill of life to travel the globe for a year (I love your pics, @Justin and Christine Lukasavige); move to New Zealand (keep going, @Carl and Cori Richards); live in an RV (@Todd Anderson, welcome back); visit the National Parks (@Ely and Kelly Pyke, your film is amazing); and take a mini-sabbatical in France to study art (inspirational, @Laurel Justice). They've rented their homes, sold off cars and motorcycles to help fund their reset, negotiated remote working arrangements, homeschooled their children while traveling the globe, and stepped boldly into the unknown to pursue their dreams. I'm so proud to know them.

Here's an entry from my friend Laurel Justice on the fourth day of her artist sabbatical in the countryside of Champagne-Ardenne, France:

> *The digs. This is home for the next thirty days—foyer, salon, bedroom. I'm overwhelmed with gratitude, to be in such a nourishing place in which my only responsibility is to create (and do my own dishes). There is a rhythm, of which I am a happy joiner: Tai Chi at 8:30, followed by meditation. Then writing, painting, drawing, practicing instruments, or whatever one's medium is, done in your own private studio in the Chateau. Then walking/hiking at 5:30; dinner at 7:00, followed by whatever late-night socializing one wants. There is a poetry night, a sharing a favorite song night, and a concert night for the musicians amongst us. So far, it's as magical as it looks and sounds.*

It does sound magical, doesn't it?

We shouldn't wait until we find ourselves terminated at work or with a cancer diagnosis to start giving heed to our unmet desires and dreams. Most of us won't be terminated or develop cancer (thank God). True, it would make the decision to get our shit together and start following our heart easier. Our feet would be forced to the flames, and we'd experience the benefit of a jolt of clarity of importance and purpose. But it doesn't have to be that way. Just ask Laurel.

Friends, when we commit to pursuing our dreams, miraculously our spiritual cells will begin to heal, reassemble, and flow life-giving nutrients back to our hearts and minds. Give your dreams room and margin to manifest into reality by starting with permission. That's right, it's okay, actually more than okay, to dream a little dream. Or why not go for a grand one? "Firing your boss" requires that you harness the power and magic of your dreams. You become friends with your dreams and learn to partner with God to live into the realization of your dreams.

Postscript: Trail running this morning, I ran into an acquaintance that scared the crap out of me. After listening to her catch me up on her life and work, I'm afraid I need to add a few guardrails to this idea of permitting ourselves to dream. I envision her reading this chapter and creating a personal permission slip to be reckless and irresponsible. Look, everything I've said here is accurate. But remember, practice non-dualistic thinking. Concurrent with these truths, if you have a family relying on you for groceries and shelter, then you need to man up (or woman up) to provide for them. To your chagrin, it may require you to work some crappy job that pays you less than you believe you deserve.

I've witnessed two evils that can quickly pervert the wisdom and stewardship behind this invitation to following our life aspirations: 1) people who want to skip doing the hard work of faithfully going to a job every day; and 2) bullshit artists selling quick fixes to make a ton of money in "three easy steps." Sometimes they're one and the same, and many are predators preying on our desperation and spirit of entitlement. We are taking an entirely different trail here and heading in the opposite direction.

The examples I've given in this chapter are dreams exercised by gainfully employed professionals (I'm feeling the urge to add a TV commercial disclaimer: "Professionals performed these stunts"). Please don't take this chapter as permission to eject on your career, stuff your wife and three kids into an RV, and follow your heart into a personal and financial crisis funded by credit cards.

The mature point I'm surfacing here is that many of us put our hands to the plow and work the field our entire life. Sadly, we never pause and smell the literal or figurative roses. We pay a personal cost for dutifully working and never allowing ourselves to pursue our dreams, even the small ones. In the next chapter, I will say more about the value of doing honorable work, but for now, let's consider this a handshake that we agree to pursue rhythm with wisdom and maturity, and a heart aroused.

CHAPTER 10

LIVING ON PURPOSE

Meaning is not something you
stumble across like the answer to a
riddle or the prize in a treasure hunt.
Meaning is something you build into your life.

—John Gardner[42]

WANTED: Eight people to participate in a life experiment with me. You qualify if:

You KNOW there is something profound and meaningful that you *want* to do with your life.

You're not sure what that profound and meaningful thing is.

You feel stuck, derailed, stalled, but aren't sure what to do differently.

You want help.

I want to help you explore your frontier, find your path, rediscover what fires you up, identify where you drifted off course, and chase down what stands in the way of limiting your experience of joy, meaning, and connection.

I TYPED OUT THIS want-ad e-mail in a moment of spiritual clarity. It was like I was receiving a direct download. I hit send, and out it went to fifteen hundred people. My proposed experiment sparked more response than any other message I've ever written. E-mails flooded in from close friends, acquaintances, subscribers, and even strangers asking to be selected as one of the experimental eight. I shouldn't have been surprised, but I was.

One immediate result of my experiment/invitation was how hungry people are. Not for literal bread, but for something more. It was clear that people are actively engaged in their work and lives, but at the same time feel completely disconnected from a reason to keep going. They just keep, well…going. What about you? Would you have been one to respond to my e-mail? You make a good living, you're being rewarded at work with more and more responsibility, but you're starving, wondering, *What's it all for? Is this it? Isn't there more?*

Those are not new questions. In fact, they're ancient. And in the spirit of the best of the ancient teachers, let's try answering questions by asking more.

Wanted: Three Questions

1. Why do we need a purpose in our lives?
2. Is our heart essential?
3. I know I'm made for more, but my job is not fulfilling.

Let's jump in, and I'll loop you back in on the lessons I learned from this life-on-life experiment.

Why Do We Need a Purpose in Our Lives? (Why Do We Need a "Why"?)

> *Those who have a "why" to live, can bear with almost any "how."*
> —Viktor Frankl, *Man's Search for Meaning*[43]

A few chapters back, I left you hanging when I shared about my daughter dying. Now that we are in the deep stuff, I'd like to go back and bring you in by telling you a story I *only* share with my friends. When Hadley was alive, every morning for twelve years Leith and I woke to a looming, anxious question needing an immediate answer: "Is she still breathing?" There toward the end, Hadley's body seemed a collection of tubes and beeps. Oxygen tubes with extended cords, feeding tubes with syringes, and electric pumps driving it all with irritating beeps that signaled her needs. But those beeps meant Hadley was still breathing. And her continued breath was our goal. As I share this with you, my heart and body flood with memories and reminders of the grief and loss, and the fun and the joy. We lived life close to the bone. Things like our car door getting dinged in the parking lot or that the Starbucks barista made my Doppio Con Panna in the wrong size cup were simply of no consequence to us. Those temporary inconveniences never landed on our prioritized list of what matters most.

"Keep her alive" became the rudder that steered our family's ship. Keeping our lives on the path of purpose and meaning was simpler then. We didn't have the interest—or the energy—to burn calories thumbing through social media feeds while growing envious about other people's above-the-waterline lives, or ranting when our candidate didn't win the presidential election. We had the gift of deeper meaning upholding the "why" of our daily lives. Friends, in full transparency, we were also physically and emotionally exhausted. It was the most rewarding and challenging time of our lives.

Then on a regular old Friday, she didn't come home from the hospital. And I lost a significant part of the reason I got out of bed every day. I lost my "why."

On the one hand, I'm grateful that most of you cannot begin to relate to my story of what it must be like to live with such an intense directive over your life. I hope you never feel that kind of pain. Although I don't miss the stress and anxiety associated with keeping our daughter alive, her cut-too-short, beautiful life taught me the importance of having a meaningful thread stitching my actions, my will, and my heart together.

Does this mean we have to go through something traumatic to find meaning in life?

Not long ago, I was introduced to American novelist, poet, and environmentalist Wendell Berry. Kentucky born and bred,

Berry spends his days close to his farmland, far from the reach of the modern world. We need watchmen to help us see, and he is one of them. In his writings, his voice serves as a welcome narrator providing clarity to the cultural collapse we're witnessing before our eyes. I especially appreciate his poem "A Timbered Choir":[44]

> *...Men, women, and children now pursued the objective*
> *   as if nobody ever had pursued it before*
> *   ...[T]he once-enslaved, the once-oppressed were now free*
> *   to sell themselves to the highest bidder*
> *   and to enter the best paying prisons*
> *   in pursuit of the objective, which was the destruction of all enemies,*
> *   which was the destruction of all obstacles, which was the destruction of all objects,*
> *   which was to clear the way to victory,*
> *   ...which was to clear the way*
> *   to self-realization, to self-creation, from which nobody who ever wanted to go home*
> *   would ever get there now...*[45]

The foil is drawn. Berry is fencing with our modern world's prescription to our soul's earnest need to find "it"—a way, a satisfying resolution to our quest for purpose. Here's the way I see it: Externally, our modern world is fickle, changing its mind frequently and growing more complicated by the millisecond. Internally, in the quiet moments alone in the shower, awake and staring at the ceiling at 2:00 a.m., or on Tuesday mornings at our desk, we're on the hunt, sniffing for a trail that will lead us to the promised land of meaning and reconcile for us the gap between the experience of our lives and our longing for connection, joy, and purpose.

The crazy thing in all this is that we already know the truth, and we know exactly what's going on even if we act like our Aunt Mildred pretending "everything's fine, just fine." Everything's not fine, but when we're drowning in the search for meaning, in the void of finding a lasting lifeline, we grasp at anything that promises to keep us afloat.

Projecting my interpretation and life experience, I conclude that we long for an anchor chain linked to a life-sustaining reason to get out of bed every morning. When we conquer our way to the finish line, focused only on ourselves, the reward for our independence and striving is perpetual wandering and never getting home. Would a summer on Berry's farm cure us of our ache? Then would we be able to find home?

Is Our Heart Essential?

If I only had a heart...
—The Tin Man

The young professional painted me a picture of his pursuit of what Wendell Berry tagged "the objective" and the "destruction of all enemies." He began his mercenary apprenticeship working for private equity firms and graduated to become a wolf of Wall

Street in mergers and acquisitions. In my mind, each of his stories represented an intricate mosaic revealing his motive behind every conversation, preemptive move, manipulation, and deal signing. They were all a growing crescendo toward: "I win by removing emotion. I have no heart." His current why is "to win, to conquer, to destroy," and like a gladiator in a Roman arena, his world roars with applause. As a recovering mercenary myself, my heart was immediately drawn to him. With a few more gray hairs than he, I've lived long enough to personally witness the aftermath of the lives of the people discarded, the careers derailed, and significant decades of loyalty squashed on the spot by the conquering party.

I asked him, "Do you know the story of the Tin Man in *The Wizard of Oz*?"

"Yes, of course."

"But did you know that he originally had a heart?"

In L. Frank Baum's books, the Tin Woodman was originally flesh and blood. He fell in love with a Munchkin girl—Nimmie Amee—the servant of an old woman, who did not wish the girl to marry and asked the Wicked Witch of the East for help. The witch enchanted his ax, causing him to cut off his body parts, limb by limb, then his heart. Without a heart, he felt he could no longer love Nimmie Amee.

"There was once a Munchkin girl in my life who was so kind and beautiful that I soon grew to love her with all my heart. She, on her part, promised to marry me as soon as I could earn enough money to build a better house for her; so I set to work harder than ever."[46] It's so important to know how the Tin Man's story began—noble, earnest, and relatable—and to appreciate that his intrinsic motive was love. Like us, he set on to work hard to accomplish a meaningful objective.

As the story goes, Dorothy and her friends encounter the sad Tin Woodman, rusty and frozen in physical form but very much alive: "The two gladly oiled the Tin Woodman's joints and freed him from his motionless existence and prison of regret and rust."[47] The quest began along the yellow brick road, as the Tin Man was off to see the Wizard to receive a new heart, aspiring to return wholehearted to his Munchkin maiden and marry her.

I wonder how many of us began with a wholehearted "why"—something intimate and specific to us—but then became locked up, immobile, imprisoned. We were headed down a right path, our career was going great, our family was healthy, and then a spot showed up on the MRI scan, or your mom suddenly stopped speaking to you, and now it's been two years of silence. Life happens, and we can find ourselves less alive and not experiencing the fulfillment, intimacy, and purpose we intended.

One of my favorite pieces of ancient wisdom comes from the biblical King David: "Above all else, guard your heart for it is the wellspring of life."[48] I've anchored to this mantra since I was fifteen years old, reminding myself that, like the Tin Man, my heart is a vital instrument that guides me in living a life rich with purpose and meaning.

Back to my conversation with Mr. I-Don't-Need-a-Heart. I shared with him:

"You can choose to keep chopping away without a heart, conquering kingdoms and taking no prisoners, and guess what? The world will reward you for it. But here's the deal. There's a cost—you will fall short of your potential. Your greatest gift to this world lies in your ability to, like the original Tin Man, operate and lead from a whole heart. The world loves you now, but I can promise you that your world will eventually tire of your heartless ways. And you? You'll rust. Maybe not today or tomorrow, but sooner than you think. The world is full of heartless mercenaries. What the world needs is more men and women courageous enough to live from a whole heart."

Our conversation penetrated his suit of armor, and he immediately softened his stout persona, speaking gently about his true loves—his wife and son. He said, "What you're saying rings true. The leader of our company (whom I look up to) has a heart, and you're right, I could never lead like he does operating the way I do." In that moment, he vulnerably admitted, "I actually do have a heart, I just don't show it at work. My love for my family is why I work so hard. I've always believed showing my humanity is weakness. I never thought it could be a strength." Mr. Tin Man's deeper purpose, anchored in the love of his family, can now be carried into his workday, allowing love, care, empathy, patience, kindness, and understanding to become imperative assets.

In the past jobs were about muscles,
now they're about brains, but in the future
they'll be about the heart.
—Minouche Shafik, London School of Economics[49]

In our careers, the temptation for some is to believe that we can get more done if we lock our hearts away at home. It's just not true. Living in this heartless way creates dissonance within us, and we rust. It takes courage to operate as a fully integrated human being at work. Living on purpose requires our intellect and our hearts working together as the instrumentation that keeps us from drifting off course. If I live from a whole heart, then will I know what my purpose is?

"I Know I'm Made for More, but My Job is Not Fulfilling"

No one needs to convince us of it. We know deep in our bones that we're made for more. But unlike all those folks on Instagram living their best lives now, some of us feel stuck, enduring long stretches of seemingly unimportant or mundane work. It is a clock-watching, soul-crushing challenge to stay engaged and feel like the work we do matters and is personally fulfilling. This disengagement and despair negatively affects us, and our hearts grow tired and weary.

For eighteen months, Leith worked the front desk at an emergency clinic. She excels at loving people, but her job wasn't fulfilling. Dutifully, she fielded phone calls from over-protective mothers, processed intake forms from senior men with sniffles (she's not a big fan of grown men who can't hack the common cold), and graciously refrained from comment when young men described their STDs.

She'd frequently return home after an eight-hour shift and, in tears, agonize over how insignificant she felt her job was. Let me be clear: She wasn't complaining. She was lamenting while she maintained her heart's song of purpose—"I want to help companies love people." Ironically, in an emergency medical clinic, her heart was growing sick. "My work feels so mundane, just sitting there. I wish I could earn money doing the things I love."

Shawn Askinosie, author of *Meaningful Work*, reminds us to keep a watchful eye for meaning wherever we find ourselves:

> *The path to vocation is smoother if we can survey*
> *the landscape in our neighborhood, work place, city,*
> *or world at large and take stock of existing needs.*[50]

Leith learned to scan past her boredom and look for opportunities to enter into authentic human connections with patients. Her end-of-day stories began to change from feeling off purpose, clock-watching, and "What am I doing and why am I here?" to on purpose in her actions: "Tell me more about your son's drug addiction." It's easy to get tripped up over whether our career is purposeful and meaningful while overlooking our ability to act purposefully within our existing role, company, and relationships. So does our job give us purpose, or does it come from within?

Life Experiment Lessons

Let me put all my cards on the table here before we attempt to land this plane. These questions about purpose and meaning are not simple, and even after reading this chapter, you'll likely have more questions than answers. I'm just as curious as you are about how to find and maintain a reason to keep going every day. When I sent that want-ad e-mail, I accepted eight people into my pro-bono life experiment. I wouldn't call it life coaching, but it was. It wasn't counseling, but in moments we went deep. These magnificent eight and I embarked on a journey over two months, scratching at these life questions together. After weeks together in individual and group exploration sessions, here are the lessons I learned.

(Let me start with an intro summary—finding purpose and meaning is a lifelong pursuit requiring constant adjustment and course-correction. Throughout life, we change and what used to turn our crank may not anymore, which means this life skill is a muscle you want to prioritize strengthening. We are hungry for something more than surviving life, and we want to experience meaning. Our culture offers a lot of temporary relief, but ultimately we find ourselves revisiting the question of "Why am I here?"

Everyone loses the trail, drifts off course, and in seasons we can find ourselves disconnected and off purpose. The art of living well is building the awareness to detect when you feel you're living on purpose and when you are ever so slightly feeling off purpose. As the previous stories illustrate, we're going to need a whole heart, and not every moment will be bliss.)

All right, here's what I learned from those magnificent eight people:

1. You have a spiritual life.

You acknowledge that there is more going on here than just "ashes to ashes and dust to dust," and you believe there is something deep and spiritual to your existence. You have spiritual wisdom that undergirds your life and reminds you that your life matters even when it sucks. You are intentional about cultivating this spiritual connection and relationship. I call this divine partnership

God. When your hope is fragile, when you need a friend, you reach out to God to supernaturally help you press through the muck of life, no matter how grim the circumstance.

2. *You take action and explore possibilities.*

You are clear about what you value in life, and you don't demand 100 percent certainty before taking action. You run experiments, try new things and, no matter how small, you take action. Maybe you point your toes in a new direction, and that is the sum of the courage you can muster. You are convinced that action equals possibility. You let go of outcomes and stop focusing on the destination. You embrace the mystery and uncertainty of the journey of life.

3. *You redefine success and failure.*

You've expanded your view of success to include joy and vitality, not just financial wealth, power, and status. You've redefined failure as impossible when you're learning lessons from every experience. You've cast off the opinions and voices of the world and choose to listen to yourself and the voice inside calling you forward.

4. *You focus on living purposefully vs. finding a purpose.*

You appreciate that discovering one life-sustaining, all-answering purpose is way too complicated and riddled with challenges. Instead, you focus your attention and intentions toward living forward by paying careful attention to your values (e.g., "be a person of integrity") and your actions. You allow a lot of grace and latitude in your self-evaluation and appreciate this is about making progress and not perfection. You've developed disciplines in your life to monitor your progress and have a few trusted allies on the journey to give you helpful feedback along the way.

Reading this, I'm grateful I conducted that experiment without receiving any financial compensation. The wisdom they helped me uncover is priceless. Thank you, Magnificent Eight.

When Hadley was alive, I couldn't see clearly that my life, my heart, and my soul were being refined. After losing her (and a big part of my "why"), I've been on the hunt for answers. To my surprise, what I've uncovered wasn't an answer so much as a new way of living. These days, we value questions over answers and prefer learning new things as opposed to resting on past accomplishments. It's really a way to care for our lives that's enabling us to successfully navigate each new day

- living with more clarity;
- experiencing deep contentment and intimate connections;
- aligning our beliefs with our actions;
- tuning out distractions.

Soulful work, no doubt, but the upside is we can keep going and living forward no matter what we encounter.

CHAPTER 11

LIVING BY DEGREES AND *TRY*

Y<small>EARS AGO,</small> I <small>WAS</small> at a low point in my burnout. Leith and I decided to attend Oprah Winfrey's "The Life You Want" tour. Oprah guided the fifty thousand attendees (mostly women) through an exercise that radically influenced the life I'm living today. She extended this invitation/challenge to us: "Think of someone you love, and think of what you want for them. Now write down what you hope for, what you dream their life could be if they went for it." This is what Leith wrote down for me. It is simple, and beautiful:

aaron...

Joy. Freedom. not a stressful job. bike job in the city for fun and fitness. driving a bmw. simple but beautiful contemporary home. low maintenance. doing podcasts. mentoring/leading prominent

141

> *business leaders and/or upcoming young ones. not*
> *carrying such a heavy weight and burden for our*
> *family. freedom to play! to rest. to live the life that*
> *you truly deeply want. joy. laughter. such incredible*
> *laughter. friendships…deep friendships.*

I'm grateful she could see what I couldn't. But as touching as that dream for me was—and it was—it felt improbable if not impossible. I simply couldn't believe in it. At the time, I was taking medication for anxiety, working eighty-hour weeks, and growing more and more disconnected from my friends and family. Leith's vision for me felt ridiculous given my headspace at the time coupled with my daily life at home and within my career. Still, despite my specific reality, I'd not lost all traces of desire. I longed to discover a future matching her prophetic vision. I pasted the copy of Leith's dream into my journal, and it served as a tangible representation of hope.

Stay Agile

Johanne Lavoie is a partner and twenty-six-year veteran at the global management-consulting firm McKinsey & Company. She is also my friend. She leads the Centered Leadership Program—a brilliant initiative, built on fifteen years of research and personal experience, helping executives deepen their self-awareness so as to create aspirational leadership visions. In the spring of 2018, Johanne cowrote an article—"Leading with inner agility"—that has become foundational for those seeking to lead companies and organizations in our new normal of constant and complex change. She points to these five personal practices to help both leaders and individuals stay agile in these transformative times. I share all five with you simply because I believe they are deserving of a much wider audience. Then I'll focus on one that has been particularly significant for me.

1. *Pause to move faster.* Pausing while remaining engaged in action is a counterintuitive step that leaders can use to create space for clear judgment, original thinking, and speedy, purposeful action.

2. *Embrace your ignorance.* Good new ideas can come from anywhere, competitors can emerge from neighboring industries, and a single technology product can reshape your business. In such a world, listening—and thinking—from a place of not knowing is a critical means of encouraging the discovery of original, unexpected, breakthrough ideas.

3. *Radically reframe the questions.* One way to discern the complex patterns that give rise to both problems and windows of emergent possibilities is to change the nature of the questions we ask ourselves. Asking yourself challenging questions may help unblock your existing mental model.

4. *Set direction, not destination.* In our complex systems and in this complex era, solutions are rarely straightforward. Instead of telling your team to move from point A to point B, join them in a journey toward a general direction. Lead yourself, and your team, with purposeful vision, not just objectives.

5. *Test your solutions—and yourself.* Quick, cheap failures can avert major, costly disasters. This fundamental Silicon Valley tenet is as true for you as it is for your company. Thinking of yourself as a living laboratory helps make the task of leading an agile, ever-shifting company exciting instead of terrifying.[51]

Amazing, huh?

Again, all five are worth your consideration, and make no mistake, they are all interconnected. But let me draw your attention to number four—*Set direction, not destination.*

Values-Based Direction

During the Centered Leadership Program, Johanne leads executives through creating a personal vision that mimics the one Leith wrote down for me—one big enough to begin living into without setting a specific destination or timeline for achievement. She believes in setting a purposeful vision and building a direction of travel rather than focusing on just objectives and arriving at a specific destination. Interestingly, she has determined that when it comes to leading ourselves, setting a values-based direction is a more effective strategy to influencing our future than picking a location on the map and driving to arrive at that destination.

Johanne and her team begin by asking direction-setting questions, such as:

• What really matters for you?

- What do you want to create through your leadership?
- What do you want to be remembered for?
- What do you want to discover?

These are coupled with questions that described the desired future state, such as:

- What will it look like?
- How will I feel?
- What will I be doing?
- What do I value and want more of?

I like to think of Johanne's advice as setting a direction rooted in purpose and meaning—the "what?" we are aiming toward. You've got to have an idea of where you want to go—not a detailed lay of the land, so to speak, but a horizon or landmark in mind: "I want to walk in *that* direction." And while an exacting plan is not helpful, any good "what?" needs an equally good "how?" or you'll end up with nothing more than a faded dream in your personal notebook.

One to Two Degrees

My lesson in "how?" came from Bill Lokey, senior clinical director at Onsite Workshops. He shares this advice if your goal is to practically make progress every day: "Start with making two-degree shifts." If you're like me, the first time I heard that I thought, "Wait, what does that even mean?" When it comes to changing the direction of our lives, the temptation is always strong to start a wide-scale off-loading of people, places, and things. Instead, this idea resembles sort of a fifty-ways-to-leave-your-lover approach, to *set yourself free*. Dear Jack, Stan, Roy, Gus, Lee, et al., please resist that temptation.

According to Bill, for most of us, our lives, careers, and relationships don't require ninety-degree, hard-right turns to get us back on track. Instead, what we need are consistent micro-adjustments in increments of one to two degrees. What this looks like are practices of continuously checking in with ourselves, pausing before we respond, saying no instead of always saying yes, listening longer, and stepping up when we want to shrink back. This principle is another example of learning to master the art of leading ourselves.

Not quite convinced of the value of two degrees? Check this: A former FedEx pilot told me that when he flew from Los Angeles to Hawaii, two degrees was the difference between arriving in Hawaii or missing the islands by eighty miles. That's right—two degrees. Now that isn't a big difference over a mile or two, but over 2,558 miles, two degrees adds up quickly and can leave you miles from your desire. Apply this truth to our lives, and it's easy to see how we can easily drift just slightly off course, and the gap compounds over miles, weeks, and years until *voila!*—we're nowhere close to where we'd hoped to be. We can experience deeper meaning and more fulfillment in our life and work by starting out with setting a values-based direction. Then, like a good pilot, faithfully make small adjustments along the way in our desired direction.

The Life I Want

Back to where I began this chapter, back at Oprah's stadium tour, when Leith wrote her vision for me.... The truth of my life then was that I was eighty miles from shore, horribly off-course, lost at sea, and nearing a tailspin due to zero fuel. But that was then, not now. Not long after that, thank God, I set a values-based direction for my life, and I've been continually making small one- to two-degree adjustments along the way. To the outside observer, those changes might not even register. But for me (and my family), they've been invaluable.

These adjustments take their form in simple ways. For example, I hold personal health as a high value, and I'm counting on feeling great when I'm eighty years old (no wheelchairs and applesauce for me). My micro-choice is pushing past my excuses and packed schedule, and I opt for a ten-minute workout instead of skipping it altogether. In my career, I've set the values-based direction that I wanted to "coach CEOs" for a living. Back when I was ladder-climbing, I gained a unique vantage point, and I developed a real heart for the unique challenges CEOs face. At first it felt ridiculous to admit my outlandish aspiration to a trusted few, for there was no visible evidence that I was qualified or equipped to help leaders. I was recovering from a burnout, needing to take a nap every afternoon, and working part time. Year by year, as I invested in becoming wholehearted and pursued my restoration and growth, little gurgles of promise surfaced, one conversation at a time.

With twenty-twenty-hindsight vision, I see how my journey of living in the trenches of corporate life, starting business units, taking products to market, laying people off, failing, ringing the bell at the London Stock exchange, burning out and coming back, all roll up to create the perfect alchemy of support for executive leadership teams. Today, I'm actively engaged with CEOs and executive leadership teams, helping support their leadership journey.

Now I can't imagine living my life any other way. I'm living the life I want. And get this—today, I'm working with Johanne Lavoie as a faculty member of the Centered Leadership Program "leading prominent business leaders," and in the dreamed-for-me-words of my wife, enjoying a lot more *Joy. Freedom...*and incredible laughter.

I haven't figured out how to be a bike courier in the city yet. But trust me, I'm headed in that direction. Those adjustments in degree are vital, and they naturally lead to my next point. None of this "life I want" would be a reality if I hadn't decided to act on the adjustments, to settle down and try, and take that first step.

You see, once upon a time, long before the Oprah tour, I believed a day would come that would hold my perfect moment. In this moment, a portal of time would open up and transport me into my desired future reality. At the time, I wanted to write books. And I wanted to be a mountain guide taking clients on an inner journey as we navigated the mountains. Sort of a Jon Krakauer character, fluent in the language of the heart. Those kinds of beliefs are fine for a child. But when I became a man, I had to put away such childish thoughts. You can spend a lifetime waiting for that perfect moment, and as Mary Oliver says, "end up simply having visited this world."

Contrary to my childish imagination, I've discovered the grown-up power in taking simple first steps of action decoupled from the pressure and demands of outcomes. Each step forward (and sometimes even back) forms a strand of DNA connected to the previous daring act or fractional tilt toward my desired destination. And yes, many days that still look like a Krakauer with a deep spiritual life.

Strong and Brave

> *I read somewhere…how important it is in*
> *life not necessarily to be strong,*
> *but to feel strong.*
> —Christopher McCandless, *Into the Wild*[52]

Years ago, my wife wanted to spark a women's movement and start her own conferences. Leith was a stay-at-home mom without a website, a platform, or a proven speaking career. In other words, she had none of what many experts deem necessary for a successful beginning. What she did have, though, was *try*. So she and a few friends decided to take those first simple steps. They determined to go for it. They'd rent a retreat center, invite women to join them via Facebook, and see what happened.

Talking about, thinking about, and dreaming about progress is important, vital even. Skipping those conversations with yourself or your team is a mistake. But they're only half of the equation. And half isn't enough. Half won't get you where you want to go. You make adjustments by degrees so you can then act. Also known as: you've gotta have *try*. Deciding and doing something different tips the dominoes of possibility, and things start moving. What Leith and I have learned is that you have to tip that first one. But how many times do we get hung up, even paralyzed, worrying about what will happen ten steps from now?

> *Far too often, we don't start because we can't get our minds around the entire thing. We don't take the first step because we can't figure out the seventeenth step. But you don't have to know the seventeenth step. You only have to know the first step. Because the first number is always 1. Start with 1.*
> —Rob Bell, *How to Be Here: A Guide to Creating a Life Worth Living*[53]

Leith and her friends hired a keynote speaker, purchased event insurance, and opened the event for registration. I'd love to tell you that forty-five women attended that first conference. But I have to tell the truth, and the truth is that *seventy-five* women came from all across the country to be a part of that inaugural Brave Beauty Weekend. Was it all smooth sailing? Not a chance. The first camp they booked flooded the week before their event. They pivoted and found another camp but then discovered that venue didn't allow alcohol for the Saturday night dance party. The decision was made to hold the Get-Your Groove-On event in our home. I wasn't there for the entire weekend, but I heard stories of amazing strength and beauty, and I did play stand-in bartender for the "Brave Beauts" celebration, which included dancing on the tables.

Remember Johanne's practice of values-based direction? You don't have to have all of the answers before you begin. Let me repeat—you don't have to have all the answers before you begin. But you do have to begin. You must take a step and commit to an inch of forward progress. Gift yourself with the reward of being tied only to the movement forward, not the outcome. Consider viewing it all as an experiment. Or maybe even an inner journey with a trusted friend into the metaphorical mountains to see what you can see.

But What If?

I recently came across this line in Patti Smith's brilliant book *M Train*. It gutted me.

> *I have always loved the ocean but*
> *never learned to swim.*[54]

I don't know the last time I've read a line that sad. She goes on to name the reason for never learning to swim. You guessed it: fear.

But what if I fail? What if it doesn't work? What if it all falls apart and people are disappointed and I'm disappointed and I lose a ton of money and my inner-critic won't stop yelling, "See, I told you so!"? Sure, all those things are possibilities. Trying something new always involves risk. We have to accept that. Always. But when it doesn't work out, that doesn't mean we're failures. Think back to my "perfect moment" when life would open up and grant all my wishes. Pretty childish, right? As grown-ups in the real world, our challenge is to ditch the childish and hold on tight to the childlike. The truth is if you try something new, you might fall down. But if you do, simply get back up. The childlike spirit reminds us all that everyone gets do-overs. We will fall short, and we can screw stuff up (sometimes royally). Welcome to the planet—that's called life. But when that life is over, you don't want to wonder if you made anything of it.

So go organize a conference.

Or write a book.

Coach CEOs.

How about learn to swim?

Don't just be a visitor.

Make those adjustments.

Decide to settle down.

And give it a try.

Try.

CHAPTER 12

YOUR LOYAL SOLDIER DESERVES THE BOOT

What we do comes out of who we believe we are.

—Rob Bell[55]

I MENTIONED THIS EARLY in the book, but after I dumped dish soap in the fish tank in biology, my high school principal informed me in disgust that I'd "never amount to anything." For a lot of years, I believed him. Based on his estimation of me, I seriously considered becoming an auto mechanic or joining the Navy instead of going to college. But I wasn't great at fixing my own car, and the Navy recruiter told me I'd be at sea for up to six months at a time with all men. No girls? Well, no thanks. So I took my chances at becoming a loser in life while attending college. And while I may not have graduated with honors, I did graduate. But for many years into my career, that high school principal's words would audibly resurface in moments when I felt in over my head and underqualified. Even though I was years removed from high school, his proclamation over my life was operationally at work within me, playing in the background of my subconscious mind and heart.

Those voices of authority in our lives, from our parents to a coach or teacher or a boss, often carry a disproportionate amount of weight in the stories we tell ourselves. They color our inner narrative, and regardless of how recent or long ago, we can still hear them say:

"Who do you think you are?"

"You don't deserve to be here."

"Who invited you?"

"Did you think this was good enough?"

"You'll never amount to anything."

It makes sense to our logical minds when the words spoken over us are undeniably harsh, cruel, and hurtful. Our emotional brain doesn't require objective facts to decipher if we should feel hurt or feel injustice. Our limbic system makes meaning out of our emotional experiences. Often it's not the words themselves that haunt us, but the meaning we interpret from a conversation, an event, or a relationship dynamic.

Box-Set Collection

Hurtful things that were said or a snide comment we overheard keep playing like tapes in our minds and hearts and, over time, influence who we become and how we show up in the world. Almost like a box-set collection of deflating hits, these messages are usually off to the side and out of plain view, yet play on an endless loop, quietly or even loudly affecting our lives and careers. They're like elevator Muzak—you don't really realize it's there until you suddenly find yourself humming along to "Sister Golden Hair." Of course, sometimes we impose these verdicts on ourselves.

A friend of mine, wholly accomplished in her career, told me a story about her and her twin sister. "She was the pretty one. I didn't want to compete with her on beauty, so I decided I'd become the smart one." Now in her late-forties, can you guess how success-ful she's been in her career? Let's just say she's incredibly successful. Second question—how does that old narrative (on repeat) impact the way she lives? Let's just say it's absolutely exhausting.

Recently, one of my coaching clients, Sarah, and I were work-ing together to explore why she wasn't experiencing the same level of fulfillment at work that she was outside of work. She works for a nonprofit organization helping combat veterans create new experiences that promote healing in the brain and body. One of her joys is leading their mountain biking program. Sounds like a great job, huh? On the surface, everything looked great. But below the waterline, she had a lot of unrest and growing disengagement.

A Tale of Two Stories

Sarah told me her career backstory leading up to that day. Along the way, she'd been a college professor, athlete, and yoga instructor. With impressive vulnerability, she said that she didn't feel smart and would often get discouraged in complex debates, with the end result being an overwhelming feeling of frustration. Plus, she couldn't stand working indoors, trapped in her cubicle eight hours every day when she could be out with clients riding bikes. Her inner narrative colluded together to sound something like this: "Something must be defective in me as everyone else seems to be better equipped for this than I am."

After listening, I asked Sarah if she realized that she told me two different storylines. She wasn't quite sure what I was talking about. The feedback I gave her was that she told one story about how she wasn't enough, felt inadequate, and was trapped in her current role, essentially waiting for someone to rescue her. The second storyline she shared, in the edges buried underneath the first story, was about her resilience, her grit, and her dynamic ability to broker peace and bring disparate people together. She had no idea about the second story.

Here's our e-mail exchange the following day. I felt it was essential to help her reframe her view of herself, her strengths, and a more empowering truth over her life:

Sarah,

I enjoyed our conversation yesterday. Thank you for being vulnerable and real.

I thought it would be helpful if I wrote out the version of the story I would tell someone if they asked me:

What is Sarah like?

What is she great at?

What makes her tick and come alive?

Sarah is incredibly sharp. She has an incredible ability to decipher meaning from complex ideas, scenarios, and piles of data. She doesn't bother herself with cataloging every component, bit and byte. Instead, Sarah has this fantastic ability to reframe the complicated into a summary that any fifth-grader could understand. Sarah can roll with academics, boards of directors, yoga instructors, snowboarders, athletes, apathetic teenagers, hard-nosed military men, and the wounded in body, mind, and soul. Sarah's kindness is a balm to anyone who encounters her. She thrives when interacting with people and advocating for change, improvement, and expansion.

She's not a big fan of oppressive, ill-fitting dogmas or endless debates that result in a winner. Sarah possesses the ability to see beyond those clashes by sincerely valuing differences and uniqueness as part of the bouquet of humanity. She's humble and curious and believes that everyone has a piece to the puzzle of the mystery of life.

She's at her best when she's met with significant challenges in a collaborative environment. She thrives on variety, action, and movement. Sarah wields a gracious, safe, and playful power within her that affects the atmosphere of every room, every conversation, and every person she interacts with. It makes sense why her yoga classes are always full and why she kicked butt as an instructor at the Community College exceeding her peer's attendance rates by double.

People want to be near and around Sarah to learn from her and to soak up goodness from her.

With such a rich depth of strengths, Sarah's career roadmap has endless destination options. Wherever she chooses to invest the fullness of herself, it's essential that she not be stuck in a corner cubicle for eight hours a day. Her energy, zeal, and influence are too valuable to be hemmed in.

Finally, Sarah is the type of person who, one brave step at a time, makes a lasting difference, improvement, and impact that receives well-deserved attention—even by Oprah Winfrey as part of her exclusive world-changers tea party (One of Sarah's life aspirations).

Sarah is soulful, valuable, influential, capable, energetic, hopeful, athletic, friendly, and a good human.

These things are right about you Sarah, and although they don't answer specifically what to do with your career today, they do address the unique value you bring to whatever endeavor you choose to invest in.

Keep going,
Aaron

A Better Story

When considering Sarah's two stories, one is obviously better than the other. And I would hope you're asking—does she just flip a switch and magically start operating from a new belief framework? How does she (and how do we) make these shifts? How do we tell (and live) a better story?

How do we move

–From: "I don't know what my purpose is (something is wrong with me)."

+To: "I'm insatiably curious and love options" (I don't know where this story is going, but it's going to be great).

or

–From: "I must be defective if I can't sit in this cubicle eight hours a day."

+To: "My energy is a super-power that shouldn't be squelched."

or

–From: "I must not be very smart. Everyone else seems to get this."

+To: "I choose to stay out of the bits-and-byte-level detail so that I can keep my eye on the big picture."

This involves exploration in a downward direction, below the surface. It requires investigating where the old stories are hiding and operating in the shadows, influencing the way we she (and we) interacts with the world. Let's pull in our trusted adviser on shame and vulnerability again and see what the research says about the power of the stories we tell ourselves. Brené Brown writes in *Rising Strong*, "The most dangerous stories we make up are the narratives that diminish our inherent worthiness. We must reclaim the truth about our lovability, divinity, and creativity."[56]

I love that word *reclaim*. It means the act of recovering something previously lost. This implies that we formerly possessed it, but it was lost, abandoned, taken, or forgotten. Remember—we are on a treasure hunt of recovering what was lost, and our freedom depends on us living into an expansive, creative, boundless future. Brené distills the magic antidote to the negative stories we've believed into three refrains:

1. "This may be the most dangerous conspiracy theory of all. If there's one thing I've learned over the past thirteen years, it's this: Just because someone isn't willing or able to love us, it doesn't mean that we are unlovable."

2. Our faith narratives must be protected, and we must remember that no person is ordained to judge our divinity or to write the story of our spiritual worthiness.

3. Like our lovability and divinity, we must care for and nurture the stories we tell ourselves about our creativity and ability. Just because we didn't measure up to some standard of achievement doesn't mean that we don't possess gifts and talents that only we can bring to the world. Just because someone failed to see the value in what we can create or achieve doesn't change its worth or ours.[57]

If we've any hope of reclaiming a better story, it begins with such reframing. This practice involves taking a good hard look at those old stories that aren't serving us any longer. Which old stories aren't serving *you* any longer? Because if the story isn't serving you, then guess what? You're serving it.

My Better Story

My mom and dad divorced when I was twelve years old. I was the oldest of three, so I quickly started assuming responsibility for my mom, brother, and sister. We were on food stamps and free lunch at school. I can remember witnessing my mom sitting at the kitchen table crying while balancing her checkbook. One Saturday morning a well-intended family friend was over at our house making some home improvements. Unplanned and organically, in the moment, he put his arm around my shoulder and said, "You're the man of the house now." Seven little words that I realize now, decades later, have fueled a lot of the drive, intensity, and care I provide for the people I love most. Let me be clear—his words weren't bad or harmful, nor are being driven and full of passion. But unfortunately, over the years, that old narrative got contorted and distorted to sound like this: "No help is coming. You're on your own. You better figure this out." If you need a visual, picture the Atlas sculpture—that man with the literal weight of the world on his shoulders. Yes, that was me.

Above the waterline, I get a lot of shit done. I'm an endurance athlete, I've experienced a lot of success in my career, and I have a beautiful family and, most importantly, a happy marriage. But below the surface, operating from that old narrative, I often felt exhausted and afraid. Afraid of what? That there would never be enough money. And exhausted from what? From always trying to prevent or control outcomes while still seeking the approval of others.

Personally, these shifts in my root beliefs have required a gradual transformation. But the journey starts for all of us with new awareness and letting go of the old. Then we can begin prototyping and exploring new possibilities. I'm not going to kid you, though, these old narratives often take time to reprogram, and that's where "practice and not perfection" becomes a perfect mantra. My friend Johanne Lavoie believes that a kinder approach to aid these shifts happens when we can "include the strength and transcend it to a more expansive place." What she means is, we can harness the strength that we've developed in response to the old narrative while moving forward without the liabilities. Let me give you an example.

So Long, Loyal Soldier

I'm driven, it's a part of who I am. But when my fear of scarcity—*there will never be enough*—is fueling my drive, I quickly become exhausted and depleted. The more expansive frontier for me is to appreciate how my drive has helped me get to where I am today while acknowledging that chances are good what got me here won't serve me well going forward. Richard Rohr brilliantly helps us here by naming this reality/character. Rohr calls it our guardian of the old narrative, our "Loyal Soldier."

Rohr believes that this kind act of acknowledging, honoring, and thanking our Loyal Soldier allows us to transition into the new expansive narrative that is awaiting us. He writes: "[We] must respect, honor, and create closure for our Loyal Soldier. We need to 'discharge' the Loyal Soldier because he or she has been in charge for most of our lives. This stalwart part of our psyche has tried to protect us, but the time comes to let it rest so that we can live more authentically in peace and freedom…. Acknowledge the ways in which Loyal Soldier has kept you safe and successful throughout your life (for example, obeying laws and staying within boundaries, repressing displays of emotion, hiding anything that would tarnish the ego's image). Offer gratitude for this great service and assure Loyal Soldier that you no longer need to be defended."

He finishes by encouraging a ritual for blessing the Loyal Soldier's dutiful service while acknowledging how he/she has restricted you from experiencing the fullness available to you. "Name some of the ways in which Loyal Soldier has had a negative, constricting effect on your life, such as keeping you from fully experiencing joy and intimacy. Speak aloud a prayer or intention: 'I choose to hear and follow the voice of Love rather than the small and confining voices of my Loyal Soldier.'"[58]

Here's my dismissal letter to my Loyal Soldier:

Dear Loyal Soldier,

Thank you for keeping me safe. Your advice and watchful whispers helped me learn to work hard and keep careful watch over the people I love most. To be fair, as much as I appreciate your wisdom, you also coerced me into taking it way too far. I worked too much, was away from my family chasing money because you convinced me that if I didn't, I might be back on food stamps again. I spent far too much energy feeling scared and not enough time enjoying my life. I love my family and friends not because you told me I should. My heart is intimately connected with the people I love, and that is who I am. I choose to invest my energy in a few things I am passionate about, and I will build in lots of time for rest and recovery. Thank you for your service, and I release you and bless you to go now. I choose to hear and follow the voice of Love.

All the best,
Aaron

P.S. I know abundance is on my side. So bugger-off scarcity!

Rohr believes that by bestowing dignity and honor on our Loyal Soldier we can, as Johanne says, "include and transcend." We continually choose to reinforce the new, more empowering, kind, and expansive truth about the person we are, the value we bring, and the nature of our signature strengths. Once the Loyal Soldier is out of the picture, we make room for fully exploring what makes us great. Telling our better story begins to sound like something from a Marvel comic. Every superhero goes through a process of realizing their signature strength, experimenting and harnessing their power to maximize their effectiveness. The same thing applies to us. For example, a handful of my signature strengths are that I am adventurous, kind, generous, humble, courageous, and I wield a lot of influence. Having released my Loyal Soldier, I'm now embracing my DNA markers and focusing on how to go big. For instance, one of my superpowers is my ability to motivate other people to do the impossible.

Quick story. Sixteen years ago, I was out running in Palmer Lake, Colorado, when I came up with this big idea to celebrate my thirtieth birthday. I blurted out to my running partner, "What if we started here in Palmer Lake and, like a triathlon, we biked, ran and climbed our way to the summit of Pikes Peak, 14,115 feet above sea level on my birthday, April Fools' Day?" And out of that blurt, the Palmer Lake to Pikes Epic—*The Epic* for short—was born. I recruited a rag-tag crew that year, and we plodded through a spring blizzard from beginning to end, finally declaring our valiant effort frozen and tuckered by Barr Camp (seven miles shy of our desired finish line).

My "sufferfest," as one friend calls it, combines the three-pronged spirit of my stylized triathlon—bike, run, hike—with the quad-busting Manitou Incline and the Pikes Peak Marathon. The real bragging rights come from its timing around April Fools' Day, regardless of weather. With every attempt, there's been rain, sleet, and snow. One year more than sixty people joined me. After five attempts, we still haven't been able to high-five on the summit of Pikes Peak. But we're getting closer, stronger, better every time.

The EPIC Route

> 2:00 a.m.: Mountain bike the Santa Fe Trail from Palmer Lake to the Bear Creek Dog Park— twenty-eight miles, three hours.

5:00 a.m.: Run Bear Creek Park to the Manitou Incline via Section 16 and Intemann Trail—eleven miles, two and a half hours.

8:00 a.m.: Hike the Incline and Barr Trail to Pikes Peak summit—twelve miles, six hours.

2:30 p.m.: Descend Barr Trail to its trailhead finish line—twelve miles, four hours.

6:00–10:00 p.m.: Finish.

In 2005, my Loyal Soldier and I co-authored "The Epic Last Will and Testament." The bones of this document I found online, attributed to "author unknown." I had every participant sign one before beginning. Check it out, it's worth a read:

ARTICLE ONE

My Compromised Intelligence

At the time of the execution of this Will, I declare to be sound of body but soft of mind, as evidence by my participation in The Epic. I further acknowledge that my desire to push the physical limitations of my own body's sane, safe, and reasonable limits is proof of my less than perfect mind. As such, if anything (like death) should happen to me as a result of this event, oh well. I've played with fire long enough; getting burned should come as no surprise.

ARTICLE TWO

The Irreparable Harm I've Caused Others

I admit that I have missed your birthdays because I had to run a marathon. Valentine's Day because I had to ice climb. And a host of other socially redemptive functions because I had to prove something to myself instead of doing something for others.

ARTICLE THREE

Enjoying My Breakfast Twice

"Why is he throwing up?" "Why does she need an IV?" These are questions the couch-sitting public loves to ask, as they generally have no idea of, or appreciation for, the often-unpalatable consequences of pushing one's body beyond the breaking point. Indeed, because I thought it was a good idea to pretend I was an endurance robot rather than a mere mortal, I remained undaunted by such questions and spectacles. And for God's sake, I was trying to do something more inspired than channel surfing, so give me a break.

This year on April Fools' Day at 2:00 a.m., the alarm blared, I peeked out the window, and it was snowing sideways again. I sent a quick text to my buddies: "Let's try again next year. Get some rest." I went back to bed and hours later I woke up and watched the snowfall from the comfort of my kitchen while sipping my coffee. Since my Loyal Soldier got the boot, I no longer have anything to prove to myself or anyone else. My drive is now under the reined harness of love and no longer ruled by the taskmaster of scarcity. I'm still motivated to complete my "sufferfest" life project, but on my new terms. Let's see what next year holds.

Oh, about my friend Sarah. She retired a few of those unhelpful tapes, and you won't be surprised to hear that within a few months of our conversation she was promoted. Under her new narrative of "I'm enough and I'm resilient and adaptive," she's taking on some new challenges. She's more focused on creating greater impact by leveraging her signature strengths and retiring those unhelpful old tapes. Adios, suckas! Hello, new world.

168

CHAPTER 13

THE POWER OF PLAY

It is a happy talent to know how to play.

—Ralph Waldo Emerson[59]

"WHEN DO YOU JUST play?" Sam's question caught me off guard. Sam was my new friend and Aloha ambassador who, just moments before, had witnessed me flip my one-man outrigger canoe repeatedly. He had graciously offered helpful advice like "try easy" and then silence to allow me some room to figure out that more muscle wasn't the answer. After a few more tries, we left the shoreline of the napping sea turtles to paddle into Kukio Bay in search of a sandy point to start our fitness routine. Onshore, running barefoot in the golden sand between push-ups and lunges, Sam dropped that question: "When do you leave your watch at home and run just for fun? When do you just play?" Between flipping the canoe and the lunges, I was feeling quite shaky. Maybe that's why he chose to ask when he did. He knew my defenses were weak, and he might get an honest answer.

Although Sam and I had just met, he knew my story. He'd met my daughter, Hadley, and he seemed to appreciate all the stress that I was attempting to manage in my life. He saw how I used physical fitness as my release valve to siphon off the built-up pressure. Having spent his career developing vacation homes along the Kohala Coast for clients with last names like Dell and Schwab, Sam knew one when he saw one—"one" being someone who didn't know how to play. In the wake of his question, I honestly had no idea what he was talking about. My answer? "Um, never."

Child's Play

We have to let go of exhaustion, busyness,
and productivity as status symbols and measures of
self-worth. We are impressing no one.
—Brené Brown[60]

Allow me to channel my inner Aloha Sam and ask you, When do you just play? When do you leave the watch, literal or figurative, behind and do something simply for the joy of it? If you, like me back then, have no idea what I'm talking about, then it's highly likely that your life is over-programmed, over-scheduled, and everything is either a competition or a checklist of efficiency or some toxic cocktail of both. If so, that's perfect. I'm here to help.

I'm intentional these days about asking people that question, "When do you just play?" And the two most popular answers I get are

1. when I'm on vacation,

or

2. never.

I don't fault anyone for those answers. They're fair. If you'll recall, "never" was the answer I gave Aloha Sam. I was truly perplexed by the idea of playing as a grown man. I needed some help interpreting what it means to play as an adult, because if I'm honest, I believed that play was for children. Thus the phrase "child's play." As kids, we played—you know, like Tonka trucks and running through the woods playing games like Capture the Flag. But in a strange twist on that old Bible verse, when I became a man, I put away those "child" things. As an adult, I was more about achieving life goals. I mean, I'm a big deal now, and there's important stuff to do, right? Of course, if anyone pressed me on the question, I'd respond with stories of climbing mountains and competing in triathlons. I assumed that because I exercised daily and occasionally came home bloody and muddy, that must mean I was playing. Yes, those were/are healthy outlets for adventure and physical fitness. But here's the subtle little secret: when I engaged in them, I was always measuring my performance, keeping score. And that's not playing.

In 1938, Dutch cultural historian Johan Huizinga wrote about the importance of play in culture: "Play is a free activity standing quite consciously outside 'ordinary life' as being 'not serious,' but at the same time absorbing the player intensely and utterly. It is an activity connected with no material interest, and no profit can be gained by it."[61] I'll spare you Johan's sociologist technical jargon. Simplified, he sees "play" as having two key qualities:

- No one is keeping score.
- We engage in an activity for enjoyment and no other gain.

Now let me channel my inner Huizinga and ask, "When was the last time you did something for the sheer fun and enjoyment of it? Seriously, when? And what do you do on a fairly regular basis that involves no element of keeping score or monitoring performance?"

Lava Rocks and Smoke Breaks

Back to that time on the Big Island. My family and I were vacationing for three weeks, which became my detox from my addictions to stress and busyness. While there, I received an invitation to join a mixed bag of men (from billionaire residents to Kona locals) for something they called "Run the Rock." We assembled on the beach, grabbed paddleboards or jumped on a five-man outrigger canoe, and splashed our way to a nearby cove for their ritual. Here's how Run the Rock goes: I partnered up with a guy, and then I'd dive down, pick up a lava rock, and run along the ocean floor. When I was out of gas, I'd resurface, and my buddy would dive down and take his turn, I mean, run. It was an absolute monster.

I later learned that running the rock is a regular aspect of lifeguard and big-wave surfer training. But I have to confess that in those moments, without a watch, void of any sense of competition, deep in the ocean blue, Sam's question clicked, and I thought, *I feel like I'm eight years old again, free from any responsibilities and fully alive down here, totally enjoying this experience! Hey, Sam, look at me, I'm playing!*

Months later, back on the mainland, at work in my office building and attempting to live with that Run-the-Rock spirit, a spark ignited: "I think I'll become a smoker." Stay with me here, okay? My reality was this—I couldn't seem to find any time during the day to play. Every minute of my work day was scheduled with calls and meetings. However, I noticed the smokers each possessed a free hall pass of permission to run outside for ten or fifteen minutes, multiple times per day. No one gave them a stink eye. Hell, there are even laws to protect them. In that realization, my idea was born—"Why don't I act like I'm a smoker and turn those workday smoke breaks into playful moments instead?"

Remember, I warned you about the necessity of holding unorthodox ideas. I'm just saying….

> *Play doesn't just help us explore what is essential.*
> *It is essential in and of itself.*
> —Greg McKeown[62]

Armed with nothing more than courage and a BIC lighter from 7-Eleven, I started using my smoke breaks to go to my truck in the parking lot and fire up my small portable backpacking stove. And for what reason? To brew up a hot cup of coffee on my tailgate. I had no intention of becoming a smoker, I just wanted an excuse to catch my breath, enjoy a few moments of not keeping score, and enter into the spirit of play. For a couple of years before this epiphany, this stove sat in my basement on my gear shelf, and it bugged the crap out of me how little use it received. I had big dreams of taking it on multi-day adventures backpacking the high country in Colorado, but I never went. Each year the stove gathered a little more dust, that is, until my brain exploded with this question: "What if I lived adventurously and played while at work?" Some men carry a lava rock underwater. Some men brew coffee during their smoke break. It's all play.

I started inviting coworkers down to my truck for meetings where they only question we had to answer was, "Do you want your coffee black or with sugar?" But that breakthrough opened up a world of possibilities for me. I began taking walk-n-talk conference calls and walking meetings on the trail behind our office. I'd get up early before work, take my fly rod to a local creek, catch a few three-inch wild brook trout before making a 9:00 a.m. meeting. I don't know if *the* world changed overnight, but *my* world sure did. Play became my secret weapon at work that transformed my daily experience of rigor and intensity into curiosity and adventure.

Okay, Aaron, but I don't fish. I don't like coffee. And the thought of running lava rocks underwater makes me light-headed. Fair enough, no sweat. Here are a few stories to help you think through ways to incorporate play in the course of your workday. The primary result is joy. But secondary benefits include reducing stress and unlocking creativity. Seriously, you'll love it!

Holding On for Dear Life and Joy in Nairobi

Here's an e-mail I recently received from a friend of mine. For years he's heard my stories of chasing the wild and finding ways to play every day. As you read his story, pay attention to his specific word choices as he describes how he felt throughout his playful excursion. Note also how tempting it was for him, and for us, to stay the predictable path and default to what we always do, like stay back at the hotel and answer e-mails. Play is the invitation to try something new and chase joy.

I went on to a work trip to Nairobi, Kenya recently. Each workday finished at 5:00 p.m., and my colleague and I would walk back to our hotel a few minutes away. The problem was, there was then very little to do in the evenings. We were not near the city center, there were security concerns about going out and about, and my colleague was not up for exploring. This was a source of frustration to me given that I had lived in Kenya before and wanted to go and explore the city. I was keen to visit a fantastic shop I had been to about ten years earlier. So, I asked the client how to get there and was told I could not take a taxi because the congestion at rush hour in Nairobi is a nightmare, and I wouldn't get there before the shop had closed. The only option was to go on a boda-boda. I asked, "What's a boda-boda?" It turns out it is a motorbike taxi you hire from some random guy at the end of the street.

So one evening, I had a choice: the predictable life of an evening of e-mails, reading, and eating in the hotel. Or, choose the life of adventure and play. So I walked up to this Kenyan sitting on a beat-up motorbike and asked if he would take me to town with the only condition being "you keep me alive!" He jumped at the chance and gave me a very-well-used helmet. I hopped on the back, and off he roared. Not being a "biker," I felt that pang of fear in my stomach after about eight seconds. Suddenly, he went around a roundabout the wrong way, wheelied up onto the sidewalk, nailed it down the sidewalk with pedestrians literally jumping out the way, bumped down onto the congested road weaving between the vehicles, and then played chicken with the oncoming traffic.

But I got into the rhythm and realized he handled his bike well. The stomach fears dissipated. He took calculated risks, and we were moving a lot quicker than the four-wheeled cars on the road. We got to chatting. He was called John and a great guy! We then hit one of those localized rainstorms—where you can almost see the column of water coming out of the sky. Soaked to the skin, we continued on and then came out into the bright sunshine again. We arrived at the shop intact, thoroughly wet, and laughing! I said, "Stay here, and when I finish in the shop, give me the grand tour of Nairobi." And that's what we did. I returned to the hotel some hours later, beaming with joy and excitement and adventure, for I had gone and seen all the places I used to visit many years before. I had the "ride of my life." I felt so alive. It made my week. And I was grateful to you, Aaron McHugh, for encouraging me to step into living a little more, playing a bit more, and enjoying the simple adventures that are there all around us!

—Ben Hines

Swooshing in Park City

After hours of business meetings, I wasn't able to make an earlier flight home to Colorado Springs. It was 3:00 p.m., and my flight didn't leave for six more hours. I sent out a tweet—"Need a micro-adventure in Salt Lake City. Help!" It just so happened that my new friend, Carl Richards, author and *New York Times* columnist, was himself boarding a flight across the runway from me and called with an idea:

"Aaron, you can go run Mt. Olympus, or you can do one of the most amazing things ever and go ride a Swiss bobsled down a snowy trail on Iron Mountain. Go to my house to pick up a sled, and my wife will give you directions."

That was all I needed to hear.

I rented a car, drove forty-five minutes, bought a pair of kid's gloves at Walmart, and waited in their driveway for Cori (Carl's wife) and her kids to arrive home. She was a great sport. I'd never even met her, but she was totally chill, like this happened all the time. She invited me in, I picked out a Swiss bob, borrowed some gear, and scratched down directions to Iron Mountain above Park City. At sunset, I started up the packed snow trail just up from the Winter Olympics circle. Once up top, I mounted the small butt-size Swiss bobsled, cranked on the headlamp, and swooshed my way down to the car. Total and complete *joy!*

Look, sure, it feels a bit weird to show up at a new friend's house when he is out of town to borrow his boots and coat, but now after discovering the joy of play, it's *more* weird to sit at the airport for four hours, drink too much, answer endless e-mails, and read *Outside Magazine* wishing I was in Belize paddling in a sea kayak.

Again, my version of play will look different than yours, and that's great. What's important is for you to focus on the question, *When do you just play?* Stop keeping score, pursue something outside of your routine life, and experience some carefree happiness within the context of your daily life. In other words, go play.

> *Play is an antidote to stress, and this is key*
> *because stress, in addition to being an enemy of productivity,*
> *can actually shut down the creative, inquisitive,*
> *exploratory parts of our brain.*
> —Greg McKeown[63]

What's in Your ~~Wallet~~ Suitcase?

I travel a lot for work, and once I unlocked this new way of de-stressing, the world became my oyster. Business travel can be a drag, but it doesn't have to be. I know—I've attended the trade shows, lectures, client dinners, training, and the like. I get it. The first step to reclaiming business travel as a playful opportunity is to remove resignation from your list of excuses. When you pack your suitcase, don't allow the resignation of "I'm only going to work" to be included. You can fulfill your work obligations and also *have a good time.* Here's my advice: Pack to play.

Here's what's in my ~~**wallet**~~ *suitcase:*

- Black Hole Duffel Patagonia 30L

- Bluffworks Jeans
- Petzl rechargeable headlamp
- Running shoes
- Patagonia Houdini jacket

And equally important, don't forget to pack the necessary mind-sets:

- Adventure awaits around every corner and in every city.
- Be curious and stay open, especially when you encounter challenges and setbacks.
- Think in small increments of time—you don't have to have an entire day. Remember, *micro*-adventures!

Now once you get there, here are five core ideas that have catapulted me into amazing playful adventures both big and small:

1. Take a break from the meeting.

More than once, I've walked the stairwell of a hotel or conference center to clear my head. I pretend I'm climbing Mt. Everest. In my imagination, the cold, concrete steps become the Khumbu Icefall above Everest basecamp. Returning to the meeting, I feel refreshed and grateful to have survived the Nepalese slopes. You get the picture. Strap on those imaginary crampons and *go*!

2. Skip dinner.

Who says you have to go out to dinner every night with coworkers? That's right, nobody. Grab a chocolate milk, a Cliff

Bar, and a banana. You're good to go for the whole evening. Visit a museum, rent a bike, and explore a city market. Skipping dinner just freed up two hours of your evening. *Go!*

3. Hire a guide.

Wherever you are, there are local guides that know the best spots. Don't waste time trying to figure out where to go and what to do. Instead, hire a guide. I've hired guides to fly-fish local rivers, surf local breaks, and kayak waterways. TripAdvisor and Yelp are my two go-to apps for "Top Ten Best Things to Do," and the guide services help make it happen. *Go!*

4. Call a friend in every city.

Think high School, college, fraternity/sorority. Now think Facebook, social media, and e-mail. Risk saying "Hey, anyone want to meet up while I'm in town?" Just last month, I hiked Twin Peaks above San Francisco and ate sushi with a buddy on twelve-hours notice. It was awesome! *Go!*

5. Find a trail nearby.

I promise you there is always a trail nearby. It may not be marked. It possibly won't be on a map. But if you'll walk outside and wander for a bit, there is always a trail, a park, an open space, or a pathway to explore. I promise. *Go!*

You can fulfill your work obligations *and* play! Seriously. While on business trips, I've explored local spots, made excursions with clients, and boarded flights home smelling like something from the underworld. Do I have my receipts, so to speak? Well, I've:

- Hiked Camelback Mountain in Scottsdale, Arizona, at dawn before an 8:30 a.m. meeting. Thanks, Uber.
- Mountain biked Altoona, Pennsylvania, trails after work with my client. She loaned me her small, pink-frame Specialized Stump Jumper. It was humbling on many levels and a total rush.
- Squeezed in a 7:00 a.m. surfing lesson in Santa Cruz, California, before meeting my Google client.
- Swum in the Pacific Ocean with Newport Coast Triathlon Team in Orange County, California.
- Discovered an old factory building converted into an indoor mountain biking park, Ray's MTB in Cleveland, Ohio, in February.

And trust me, I could go on and on. All made possible by a simple but powerful question asked by a wiser, older human: *When do you just play?*

The point of all this is that if we're going to go the distance in our careers (and most of us work too much and live our lives too little), we're going to need to reclaim *play* as a vital partner. Don't miss that word: *vital*, as in "of utmost importance." You can personalize your form of play, like making a cup of coffee on the roof of the apartment building you manage (keep going, @Jake Blakeney); launching from your backyard and kayaking downriver to catch the sunset (killer, @Matthew Curtis); lassoing a trash can on the balcony of your office building (thanks for the video, @Bryan Byrd); or flying a kite at the beach and visiting a park at lunch (loved the stories, @Russ Long). Again, I could go on and on.

See, I told you firing your boss was going to be fun! *Go!*

CHAPTER 14

PACE YOURSELF

The best asset we have for making a
contribution to the world is ourselves.
If we underinvest in ourselves, and by that,
I mean our minds, our bodies, and our spirits,
we damage the very tool we need to make our highest contribution.

—Greg McKeown[64]

"IT'S THE AGE OF Anxiety," proclaimed the TV reporter cutting through the white noise of my Saturday morning chores. My first response was, *Really? Is that the banner that we as humans are living under today?* I allowed the question to drop so that my heart could reflect on aspects of my life, my community, and the world I encounter outside my front door. Yep, I agree our world is a bit of a shit show. I don't want to throw a bunch of stats out here about how America is among the top three most medicated, depressed, and overworked countries in the world, but it is. Look it up for yourself. The trajectory of this gets worse. In Japan, thirty-one-year-old journalist Miwa Sado died with her cell phone in hand. What was her cause of death? *Karoshi*—Japan's name for death resulting from chronic overwork which is responsible for taking the lives of thousands each year.[65]

Three miles per hour—that's the speed at which we humans *used* to live. Since the beginning of time, man walked everywhere under the power of our own two feet. Our pace of life was symbiotically linked to our pedestrian mode of travel. We lived and worked in villages and hamlets, strolled to sip beers at the pub, ambled to our places of worship, and we lived our lives within a fifteen-mile radius, never venturing far from our own backyard.

For our modern world, that's an incomprehensible idea. However, for millions of years, our genetic code programmed us for living at much slower rhythms. Our sauntering life sped up overnight in 1804 with the invention of the steam train, and suddenly life could be experienced at top speeds of 125 mph wherever man could lay down escape tracks. Insatiably curious, fifty years ago we pushed our quest to include the stars, and man left the confines of terra firma and rocketed away at 24,791 miles per hour to meet the man in the moon.

Pause for a second and let's pull in mythic truth again and reflect on the predicament this has created for us as human beings. For millions of years, our genetic engineering predisposed us to live a hobbit's pace of life, and yet our world today is demanding that we live at Mach-10 speeds. Transportation's jump to light speed is the perfect metaphor to contrast our inability to live beyond our three-mile-per-hour origins. Be honest with yourself—how much longer can you keep participating in the Age of Anxiety, earning the merit badges of hurry—over-scheduled, over-programmed, and overwhelmed—before you, well, burn out?

For three decades, Olympic gold medalists, military special forces, hostage rescue teams, surgeons, and Fortune 500 CEOs have been the subjects of study at Johnson & Johnson's Human Performance Institute. This is the question they've been probing: How well are we humans navigating this exponential change and paradox of pace, choice, and human potential? Their conclusion? "Technology and society have changed faster in the last fifty years than any other time in history. Many of these new elements of life interfere with our ability to meet life's challenges by taxing our attention, strength, and stamina, resulting in a "human energy crisis," which leads to fatigue, disengagement, judgment errors, stress, and burnout."[66]

By way of story, I'd like to hold up a mirror enabling you to reflect on your own life and way of working. My hope is that you will see a few things in yourself that may be contributing to your inability to achieving your highest potential.

> *With remarkable consistency, these executives tell us*
> *they're pushing themselves harder than ever to keep up*
> *and increasingly feel they are at a breaking point."*
> —The Energy Project[67]

Jen Fisher

Meet Jen Fisher. She's an executive, wife, friend, daughter, and go-getter. Five years ago, like a marathoner on mile twenty-two of a racecourse, she hit the figurative wall—her energy crisis. Outwardly, everything was going great. She was a rising star in her career choice. But in the engine room of her life, things started to misfire. I had a conversation with her, and she vulnerably shared her struggles, the messages from her Loyal Soldier, and her inability to live at the speed of light.

What qualifies you to help others avoid and recover from burnout?

I was always on, constantly connected, and in my mind, if I worked twenty hours a day, got a couple of hours of sleep, and went to the gym for an hour each day, I was golden. I could handle it. I was balanced. I had all the well-being in the world that I needed.

Did your family and coworkers see it coming?

The way I was living and working started to wear on me in different ways, and the people who care about me and my life tried to bring their concerns to my attention. I think most notably my husband, but we never liked to be told those things by our spouses. So, of course, I denied it, and I didn't want to accept it. I think partially because to me, that meant failure. It said that I couldn't handle all of these things. I couldn't be everything to everyone at all times. In other words, I couldn't be a superwoman.

What was the hard advice that you received?

I got promoted, and I remember having conversations with my new boss asking what exactly I would be doing in my new role. She said, "Well, the first thing that you're going to do is take some time off, and you're going to figure out who Jen Fisher wants to be." In my mind, I thought, "Well, what does she mean? I don't need time off. I'm ready to dive into my next role. I'm ready to go. I want to knock it out of the park." But in reality, I did take some time off. I went to bed, and I actually didn't get back out of it for three weeks. Everybody had tried to tell me, and they were right. I was mentally, physically, and emotionally exhausted.

Who did Jen Fisher decide she wanted to be?

I had to completely change and redefine myself. I had to learn to listen to both my body and my mind in order to figure out what was *necessary*. That way I could continue to excel in my new role but also excel in my life and be present for the people that matter to me.

What can we do to prevent burnout?

The more real we can get with ourselves and each other, and develop the courage to do less—that's an incredible way for us to stop burnout in its tracks. But you have to be self-aware, and you have to be willing to accept that you can't do everything. You can't be a superwoman or a superman. But you can be human. It's okay because you have a long life to live and not everything has to be done right now—especially if you're sacrificing yourself.

How did you develop the courage to do less?

Instead of saying, "I can't say no," ask yourself, "Why am I saying yes to this?" or "Why do I feel like I need to say yes to this?" Stop for a second and, instead of pushing the accept button, ask, "Is this the right thing to do? Is this the right way to be spending my time? Is there someone else that can help with this? Do we really need to be doing all of these things, and (here's a tough one) just because we've been doing it this way for the past fifteen years, do we need to continue to keep doing it this way?"

What path are you on today?

Today, I lead the crusade for personal well-being and improving work-life balance as the chief well-being officer in the US at Deloitte. I'm committed to driving the strategy and innovation around work-life, health, and wellness to empower our people to be well so they can perform at their best in both their professional and personal lives.

I love Jen's phrase about "developing the courage to do less." Imagine being healthy, confident, and well balanced enough to courageously

- quit that committee you keep attending because of guilt;
- opt out of that ninety-minute weekly meeting you're not contributing to;
- resist signing up to deliver the big presentation because you're afraid of what your boss will think.

Can you see the places in your life where you're attempting to be superwoman or superman? What else do you need to stop doing? Or start doing *less* of?

Friends, our workplace experiences and life experiences would feel massively different if we too became courageous enough to do what Greg McKeown calls "less, but better." When we begin to view our life as one big energy-management project, then we are forced to grapple with our limitations and the reality that we can't do it all. Doing so allows us to fully invest our "yes" in far fewer places.

Unplug. Reboot.

In 2015, I found myself in burnout with a side of "I can't do this anymore." I was attempting to muster the courage to call my CEO and tell him, "I need to take a four-month medical leave of absence to recover my life." My friend Tess Vigeland, a former NPR broadcaster, sent me a handwritten note that included this quote from Ann Lamott:

> *Almost everything will work again if you unplug it for a few minutes, including you.*

I pushed past my fear and the feelings of shame and prioritized my own wellness, admitting to myself, *I can't do this.* I made the call, and I'm grateful to say that my boss was incredibly supportive. Leading up to burnout, I was on the top of the world, repeatedly promoted, with stock options waiting to vest. But what good is being on top of the world if you're out of gas? My physical body felt like a network of surging electrical current without an off switch. Describing my Age of Anxiety symptoms to a friend, I confessed, "It is as if my bone marrow—the deepest part of me—is depleted. It's worse than adrenal gland fatigue. My emotional energy cells are Death Valley dry." Now I had four months to find out what went wrong and how to begin to live at a more sustainable pace.

Emotional Calories

Weeks into my leave of absence, I visited a friend wheelchair-bound by a rare chronic fatigue disease. She shared how her illness required a degree of shrewdness I'd never considered. "I have to budget my energy to do small things like grocery shopping." That was an *aha!* moment for me. I knew what I had to do. I too had to become clever and cunning in my ability to budget my intake of nutrients and my output of energy. I started breaking down my life and work experiences into two simple energy hemispheres:

+Nutrients: The stuff that fills me up—energy coming in.
–Depletion: The thing that burns my energy—energy going out.

As an endurance athlete, I'd spent decades calculating how many calories of nutrition I needed to power my desired energy output. For example, to complete an Ironman triathlon I determined I needed to intake around 200 calories of nutrition per hour to complete the 2.4-mile swim, 112-mile bike, and 26.2-mile run. I applied this simple idea of intaking caloric nutrients into my life and named them "emotional calories." I started plotting my daily activities, broken down like a packaging label of nutritional facts:

Activity: 100 unread e-mails
Calorie requirement: 200 emotional calories to power the activity
Available energy: 100 emotional calories
Choice: Read the most essential 50 e-mails and leave the rest

Get the picture? No? Let me elaborate a bit more.

Nutrients

Do you know what fills your tank? I find a lot of people know what zaps their energy, but many find it perplexing to write down a quick bullet list of the things that bring them life. Start simple, like taking the dogs for a walk or a cup of coffee in the morning before everyone is awake. For my son, it's listening to music when everyone is asleep (aka 2:00 a.m.).

For me, I started with four things:

• A trail run

- A glass of wine with my wife
- Time alone
- A conversation with a good friend

In the middle of burnout, I realized that I'd neglected the activities, rituals, and relationships that contribute to filling up my emotional energy tanks. To nurse myself back to health, I started adding nutritional values in the form of a calorie count of goodness. Take a look at my list as an idea starter for you to make your own list. Notice that the nutritional value of spending time with a good friend (+300 emotional calories) and watching Netflix for an hour (+200 emotional calories). Both provide nutrients, but spending time with a good buddy is like eating an avocado, whereas vegging in front of the TV is more like eating a Snickers bar.

Nutrients to fill me up	Calories
Emotional	
+ Time with my family	300
+ Good food and a glass of wine with my wife	300
+ Adventure	400
+ Laughter	100
+ Being with good friends	300
Mental	
+ Meditation	200
+ Doing work I love	500
+ Reading a book	300
+ Watching Netflix for an hour	200

Physical

+	Rest and sleep	800
+	Going for a trail run	300

Spiritual

+	Prayer and time alone with God	300
+	Quiet	300

Calorie Depletion

Now let's take a look at the stuff that drains us and takes energy away from us emotionally, physically, mentally, and spiritually. You'll see in my list below the stuff that zaps my energy:

- Hurried pace of life
- Over-scheduled calendar
- Disagreement with a friend
- Twelve-plus-hour workdays

When I first started practicing this ritual of assigning caloric burn rates to my activities, I was operating at a deficit every day. The number of situations, people, and circumstances that depleted my energy far outweighed the amount of nutrients I was consuming. This explained why I felt exhausted most days. Using this idea over time, I was able to create a healthy and sustainable diet of nutritional calories coming in to support my energy going out.

Emotional Calories as Expenditures	Calories
Emotional	
– Difficult client conversation	300
– Hurried paced of life	400
– Business travel longer than three days	400
– Disagreement with a friend	400
Mental	
– Overscheduled back-to-back meetings	300
– One hundred new unread e-mails	200
– Endless to-dos	150
– Having an intense debate with colleagues	300
Physical	
– Lack of sleep	400
– Twelve-hour workday	500
Spiritual	
– Letting an employee go	500
– Being with people 24/7	300

Now apply your (+) nutrient intakes side by side with your daily (–) expenditures, just like you would build a diet plan using a daily goal of 2,000 calories (think of an endurance athlete in the race of life).

Here's a quick snapshot of how I plan my days to intake enough nutrients to support the caloric expenditures I know I will need to power my day.

+ Emotional Calories as Nutrients		– Emotional Calories as Expenditures	
Morning run	300	Twelve-hour workday	–500
Good night's sleep	800	Slept only five hours	–400
Doing work I love	500	Overscheduled back-to-back	
Meditation	200	meetings	–400
Thirty minutes of quiet	300	Difficult client conversation	–300
Being with a good friend	300	One hundred unread e-mails	–200
	Total 2400	Ninth week in a row of	
		business travel	–600
		Total –2400	

Do you see how ridiculous it is for us to attempt to relentlessly work sixty-hour weeks, say yes to everyone and everything, and always pretend we're showing up as our best selves? Looking back now, I see how I was fooling no one, including myself. The upside of budgeting your energy is that it allows you to create renewing rituals so you can deliver optimal results consistently. Reclaiming the spirit of a three-mile-per-hour existence will allow you to experience more joy, connection, intimacy, and well-being.

Here are a few bite-size recommendations for daily snacks (positive emotional calories):

- Schedule twenty-five- and forty-five-minute meetings instead of thirty-minute and sixty-minute meetings.
- Take walking meetings, otherwise known as "walk-n-talks."

- In between meetings, schedule rest breaks of ten to fifteen minutes on your calendar. Title them "Planning" or "Strategy" sessions.
- Practice meditation using apps like Headspace and Calm. Dan Harris, ABC news correspondent who had a panic attack on live television and author of *10% Happier,* promises that "meditation won't solve all of your problems, but it will make you 10 percent happier."[68]
- Schedule *snack* times: Make a phone call to friend, shoot a text, go for a walk, or listen to your favorite song.

Lessons from a Monastery

In 2018, I spent a week attending training to become a facilitator of transformation. I lived at a monastery and took part in the daily rhythms of life with the brothers. Here's what I wrote in my journal:

> *I'm listening to a rooster crow outside my window on this foggy morning in the Netherlands. The monastery I'm staying at has a daily rhythm, giving continuity to each day—the rooster crows, the coffee brews, a meal is served, and a moment of silence is observed.*
>
> *There is purposefulness to every routine. I watched a young man with Down syndrome dutifully sweep cobwebs from the foundation of the building. My soul finds delight in this pace and intentionality of life. When my interior life—my*

desire for rest and ease—finds a habitat that matches my insides, I feel at home.

Lessons I can bring home with me:

- *Observe a moment of silence before every meal.*
- *Take a quiet moment during the day to walk outside.*
- *Recognize and acknowledge I have everything I need right now.*

In a nutshell—*know yourself.* Become a student of how you operate best. No one else is going to do this, and it's not their responsibility anyway. It's yours. Learn how you work best so that you can make your highest impact and contribution in work and life. Don't wait until you're on the bench of life having to take a time-out because you allowed the Age of Anxiety to leave you bankrupt. Decide to live in a different age—maybe the Age of Thriving. Or the Age of Flourishing. Then again, it might be choosing to live at a different pace—something much more human, something about three miles per hour, maybe a little more, or less. Pace yourself.

CHAPTER 15

DOING THE DEED

I PROMISED YOU FROM the beginning that we had to take a long way round to get to this point of firing your boss. We started with the realities that help is not on the way and no one is coming to save you, but you can choose who you want to be in the world. Now you are ready to do the deed and fire your boss. I invite you to find a mirror and look yourself in the eyes. I'm totally serious. It won't be the same if you just read this quietly to yourself. Go find that mirror and look yourself in the eyes.

Now picture your boss's face, and repeat after me:

> (Insert your boss's name), I am herby notifying you that I am retiring from my old way of working. I'm done with being ruled by Fear and Self-preservation. They are no longer my masters. I've recruited Abundance and Freedom to be my career guides from here on. The prospects of my future are limitless, and I release you from

the responsibility of inspiring and motivating me to do great work. I am accountable for my engagement at work and within my life. I'm sorry that I put that pressure on you before. I alone am the captain of my soul, and you are not responsible for my future. I am not quitting. I know quitting won't resolve my deeper unrest, but I am giving you notice that things will be different around here. I'm cultivating new internal realities that will find expression externally in the way I work. I choose to stand up, be counted, and contribute a verse to the great play.

For starters, I am no longer capable of following all of the rules. That's right—I've become a heretic, and it is time for me to make a ruckus here. I'm tired of playing it safe, coloring inside the lines, and heeding all of the false warnings. I've hopped a few of those fences and explored the wild side, and I discovered that I possess something unique within me that I'm obligated to bring to the world. I'm not waiting on you to give me permission to do great work and invest my best. You no longer hold the verdict on the value of my contribution—I do. I am on a quest to flush out exactly what my gifts are, and I'm finding new clues every day.

I choose to believe again in mythic truth like I did when I was young and embrace the mysteries of things I cannot see with my eyes but I know in my heart. I am retiring from reacting to my circumstances and the feeling like my vote doesn't count. I will stop cashing my paychecks if I disagree with my working arrangement, and I permanently retire from using the blame card. When faced with the question, "What's wrong with the world?" I start with self-evaluation to consider what contribution I am making to the challenges I'm experiencing. I apologize for the unproductive and unhealthy ways I've taught you to treat me. From this moment on, I'm going to be making some changes to what I expect and need from you.

Now that you're on a roll, *keep going*!
Keep looking in the mirror, and fire your company.
Fire your team.
Fire your employees.
Fire your clients and your colleagues.
And then say this:

You will see me leading as a revolutionary, helping improve our workplace. When I see my colleagues disengaged and on the slippery slope of apathy, I will throw a flag on the field and say, "What the hell are you doing? Life is too short and you're too valuable to show up to life like this."

Going forward, I am empowered to create, innovate, dream, and experiment my way toward a future I want to be part of. I'm turning my ear toward the advice of my younger guides. There was great advice there in the beginning that I know will help me today. Thank you for the lessons that you've taught me—all the good ones and all the lessons from the lair. My heart wrote them all down. You are not responsible for creating purpose and meaning for me. I'm on a quest to figure that out for myself. I may not know exactly what my big purpose in life is yet, but I'm making constant two-degree adjustments and tilts, running life experiments, and paying attention to when I feel on and off purpose.

Starting today, I choose to invest my passion and my whole heart at work. I know that I live in a mercenary world, but while achieving great things, I can operate from a missionary heart, enabling myself to be grounded in more meaningful objectives than just making another buck. Plan on witnessing me as more human at work. Count on it.

I dismissed my Loyal Soldier from calling all of the shots, and now I've reframed my inner narrative to include his strengths and transcend into more expansive and more empowering possibilities.

Those unlived lives within me? I'm giving them voice and space to become my reality. So don't be surprised if I ask for an excessive amount of paid time off, a sabbatical, and, heck, maybe even every Friday off for the summer. I can no longer allow my dreams and passions to sit on the shelf. I've notified Resistance: "I'm coming for you."

I picked up the habit of smoking, and I'm entitled to two daily ten- to fifteen-minute smoke breaks. I'll be sneaking outside to take a walk, catch some fresh air, and maybe even brew up a cup of coffee in the parking lot. I'm going to be leveraging the power of play every day. Trust me. I'll come back more creative, rested, and charged. My advice? Just go with it and don't ask many questions.

Finally, I'm not a robot, and I will no longer say yes to every project, every need, and every emergency that arises. I will be investing my limited emotional, physical, mental, and spiritual energy strategically to maximize the impact of my work and life. If you see me with my headphones on and my eyes closed, just come back in ten minutes. I'm meditating and giving myself an emotional-calorie snack time to recharge.

Thanks for everything.

You're fired.

Awesome! One more to seal the deal—repeat after me:

Now I am free.
I am the director of Success and Happiness of my life.
I am the CEO of My Life Inc.

I am the chairman of the board for my future.

I am the boss of me.

Okay, catch your breath, wipe away your tears of joy, and let it settle in. You did it. It is finished. Actually, it's just beginning because once and for all, you've punched fear in the face, and now your bright future can be realized. Do you remember the boss I talked about back in the first chapter? The day I fired her, I liberated us both on the same day. Now if I had actually said out loud what I desired or supposedly needed from her, I would have been the one being fired.

But in firing her, we both became free to operate under a new arrangement. I was no longer living under the tyranny of self-preservation. I was no longer signing the unwritten contract and being frustrated about my compliance with it. I was no longer worried about whether or not I got a pat on the back, and I wasn't waiting around for permission to start creating and innovating. And she no longer had to listen to my speeches about how she should change the way things were.

The Result

My boss loved what I started offering and the leadership I started providing, and, ironically, she was more appreciative of me. In the end, we ended up in a partnership arrangement.

I had a new job, and I didn't have to quit my job to get it. And here's the kicker: she never knew what changed.

Wait until she reads this and finds out that I fired her.

EPILOGUE

29 April, 2019

TODAY, AS AN AFFILIATE advisor to McKinsey & Company, I spend time with some of the most influential leaders in global business, helping them maximize their impact in the workplace while leading with a whole heart. None of this would be possible for me today had I not started transforming into the kind of person who can creatively lead myself. I'm a work in progress and under constant renovation (no doubt), but *Fire Your Boss* is the daily mantra that reminds me of who is accountable for my engagement, contribution, satisfaction, impact, and future. I am.

Don't forget that when it comes to you—*you* are.

Keep going,
Aaron

Curious about me?

Find my body of work at aaronmchugh.com, and my *Work Life Play* podcast wherever you subscribe.

ENDNOTES

1   "The Matrix/Quotes," Matrix.Fandom.com, accessed June 2,
    2019, https://matrix.fandom.com/wiki/The_Matrix/Quotes.
2   Gallup Daily: U.S. Employee Engagement," Gallup,
    accessed June 2, 2019, https://news.gallup.com/
    poll/180404/gallup-daily-employee-engagement.aspx.
3   "Engaged Employees Less Likely to Have Health Problems,"
    Gallup, December 18, 2015, https://wellbeingindex.
    sharecare.com/engaged-employees-less-problems/.
4   Dylan Love, "Steve Job's 13 Most Inspiring Quotes,"
    Inc., April 15, 2014, https://www.inc.com/dylan-
    love/steve-jobs-most-inspiring-quotes.html.
5   William Ernest Henley, "Invictus," Poetry
    Foundation, accessed June 2, 2019, https://www.
    poetryfoundation.org/poems/51642/invictus.
6   Hugh MacLeod, *Evil Plans: Having Fun on the Road to
    World Domination.* readitfor.me, Book Summary, 4.

7   Annamarie Mann and Jim Harter, "The Worldwide
    Employee Engagement Crisis," Gallup: Workplace, January
    7, 2016, https://www.gallup.com/workplace/236495/
    worldwide-employee-engagement-crisis.aspx.

8   Jim Harter, "Employee Engagement on the Rise in the
    U.S., Gallup: Economy, August 26, 2018, https://news.
    gallup.com/poll/241649/employee-engagement-rise.aspx.

9   Bill Burnett and Dave Evans, *Designing Your Life: How to
    Build a Well-Lived, Joyful Life* (New York: Knopf, 2016), 28.

10 Henley, "Invictus."

11 Oluwaseunfunmi Bolarinwa, "Here's the Number
    One Reason 8 out of 10 Businesses Fail within the
    First 18 Months and Why Only 50% Survive the
    First 5 Years," LinkedIn, January 22, 2018, https://
    www.linkedin.com/pulse/heres-number-one-reason-
    8-out-10-businesses-fail-within-bolarinwa.

12 Burnett, 28.

13 Marin McCue, "The Hero's Journey Chart,"
    Dopeame.com, May 16, 2016, http://www.dopeame.
    com/blog/2016/5/16/the-heros-journey.

14 "The Matrix Quotes."

15 Seth Godin, "I quilt," *Seths.blog*, April 21,
    2010, https://seths.blog/2010/04/i-quilt/.

16 Frank Sonnenberg, "The Biggest Mistake, Ever!"
    Frank Sonnenberg Online, October 6, 2105,
    https://www.franksonnenbergonline.com/blog/
    the-biggest-mistake-ever/?platform=hootsuite.

17 Randall Beck and Jim Harter, "Managers Account
    for 70% of Variance in Employee Engagement,"

Gallup: Business Journal, April 21, 2015, https://news.gallup.com/businessjournal/182792/managers-account-variance-employee-engagement.aspx.

[18] "Most Creative People 2011: Sunni Brown," *Fast Company,* accessed June 2, 2019, https://www.fastcompany.com/person/sunni-brown.

[19] Al-Anon Family Groups of South Carolina, https://www.al-anon-sc.org/the-family-disease-of-alcoholism.html.

[20] Mahatma Gandhi, "Mahatma Gandhi Quotes," Goodreads, accessed June 2, 2019, https://www.goodreads.com/quotes/50584-your-beliefs-become-your-thoughts-your-thoughts-become-your-words.

[21] Walt Whitman, "O Me! O Life!" Poets.org, accessed June 2, 2019, https://www.poets.org/poetsorg/poem/o-me-o-life.

[22] Norman Maclean, *A River Runs Through It and Other Stories* (Chicago: The University of Chicago Press, 2017), 4.

[23] Mike Rowe, "What Is the Business Case for Generosity?" *Fast Company*, March 2, 2012, https://www.fastcompany.com/video/mike-rowe-what-is-the-business-case-for-generosity/zNXJFVXM.

[24] "*Jerry Maguire,*" Wikiquote, accessed June 2, 2019, https://en.wikiquote.org/wiki/Jerry_Maguire.

[25] Leadership Circle Profile Interpretation manual TLC 10.1

[26] "What's Wrong with the World?" Chesterton.org, April 29, 2012, https://www.chesterton.org/wrong-with-world/.

[27] Heather Hurlock, "Two Lessons on Blame from Brené Brown," *Mindful*: Well-Being, August 4, 2017, https://www.mindful.org/two-lessons-on-blame-from-brene-brown/.

28   Bob Anderson, "The Spirit of Leadership," p. 24,
     The Leadership Circle: White Paper, accessed June 2,
     2019. http://2y3l3p10hb5c1lkzte2wv2ks-wpengine.
     netdna-ssl.com/wp-content/uploads/2019/04/Spirit-
     of-Leadership-Whitepaper-V.2-MAR2019.pdf.

29   Asad Meah, "50 Inspirational Nelson Mandela
     Quotes That Will Change Your Life," Awaken The
     Greatness Within, accessed June 2, 2019, https://
     awakenthegreatnesswithin.com/50-inspirational-
     nelson-mandela-quotes-that-will-change-your-life/.

30   Fred Shapiro, "Who Wrote the Serenity Prayer?"
     The Chronicle of Higher Education, April 28,
     2014, https://www.chronicle.com/article/
     Who-Wrote-the-Serenity-Prayer-/146159.

31   Rob Bell, Two-day business leaders
     workshop, Laguna Beach, CA, 2015.

32   Bronnie Ware, "Regrets of the Dying,"
     BronnieWare.com, accessed June 2, 2019, https://
     bronnieware.com/blog/regrets-of-the-dying/.

33   Herb Scribner, "Here's How Many Millionaires There Are
     in the U.S.," *Des Moines Register*, March 24, 2018, https://
     www.desmoinesregister.com/story/life/features/2018/03/24/
     heres-how-many-millionaires-there-are-in-the-us/33205747/.

34   Cameron Huddleston, "Why Happy People Earn
     More Money," *HuffPost*, last updated October
     8, 2017, https://www.huffpost.com/entry/
     why-happy-people-earn-mor_b_8038640.

35   Benedict Carey, "The Fame Motive," *New York Times:
     Psychology*, August 22, 2006, https://www.nytimes.
     com/2006/08/22/health/psychology/22fame.html.

36   Jason Reitman, *Up in the Air* (Hollywood,
      CA: Paramount Pictures, 2009)

37   Matthew Love, "10 Revelations from the Jim Carrey-
      Andy Kaufman Doc *Jim & Andy: The Great Beyond,*"
      New York: Vulture, November 17, 2017, https://
      www.vulture.com/2017/11/10-revelations-from-
      the-new-jim-carrey-andy-kaufman-doc.html.

38   Ibid.

39   Steven Pressfield, *The War of Art: Break Through the Blocks
      and Win Your Inner Creative Battles,* (New York: Rugged
      Land, 2002), Kindle ed. - Location 106 of 1223.

40   Fr. Richard Rohr, "The Dualistic Mind," Center
      for Action and Contemplation, January 29, 2017,
      https://cac.org/the-dualistic-mind-2017-01-29/.

41   Pressfield, Location 106 of 1223.

42   John Gardner, "Personal Renewal" speech, delivered
      November 10, 1990, PBS.org, http://www.pbs.org/
      johngardner/sections/writings_speech_1.html.

43   Viktor Frankl, Man's Search for Meaning
      (Boston: Beacon Press, 2006), Foreword.

44   Copyright © 1998 by Wendell Berry, from "A Timbered
      Choir." Reprinted by permission of Counterpoint Press.

45   Wendell Berry, "A Timbered Choir," Look & See, accessed
      June 2, 2019, https://lookandseefilm.com/poems.

46   Larry Spring et al., "Tin Woodman," OzFandom.com:
      Oz Wiki, https://oz.fandom.com/wiki/Tin_Woodman.

47   Ibid.

48   Proverbs 4:23.

49   "Minouche Shafik," Alain Elkann Interviews,
      April 1, 2018, http://www.alainelkanninterviews.

com/minouche-shafik/?fbclid=IwAR3jd61l9jul_
lJSqPkbqwOAOcz9OLlXDyw0xA_1LWuhZ8IKX2KSN3VerYg.

50   Shawn Askinosie, *Meaningful Work: A Quest to Do
Great Business, Find Your Calling, and Feed Your
Soul* (New York: TarcherPerigree, 2017), 14.

51   Sam Bourton, Johanne Lavoie, and Tiffany Vogel,
"Leading with Inner Agility," *McKinsey Quarterly,* March,
2018, https://www.mckinsey.com/business-functions/
organization/our-insights/leading-with-inner-agility.

52   *Into the Wild,* (Hollywood, CA: Paramount Pictures, 2007).

53   Rob Bell, *How to Be Here: A Guide to Creating a Life
Worth Living* (San Francisco: HarperOne, 2016), 93.

54   Patti Smith, *M Train* (New York: Knopf, 2015), 129.

55   Rob Bell, *Sex God: Exploring the Endless Connections
Between Sexuality and Spirituality* (Grand
Rapids, MI: Zondervan, 2008), 145.

56   Brené Brown, *Rising Strong,* (New York:
Spiegel & Grau, 2015), 82.

57   Brené Brown, "The Most Dangerous Stories We Make Up,"
BreneBrown.com, July 27, 2015, https://brenebrown.com/
blog/2015/07/27/the-most-dangerous-stories-we-make-up/.

58   Fr. Richard Rohr, "Discharging Your Loyal Soldier,"
Richard Rohr's Daily Meditation, May 3, 2014, https://
myemail.constantcontact.com/Richard-Rohr-s-Meditation-
-Sabbath----Discharging-Your-Loyal-Soldier--A-Ritual.
html?soid=1103098668616&aid=RgsDQQxIaL4.

59   Ralph Waldo Emerson, *Emerson in His Journals*
(Cambridge, MA: Belknap Press, 1984), 138.

60   Brené Brown, *Dare to Lead: Brave Work. Tough Conversations.
Whole Hearts* (New York: Random House, 2018), 106.

61   *"Homo Ludens,"* Wikipedia, last updated April 25, 2019,
https://en.wikipedia.org/wiki/Homo_Ludens.

62 Greg McKeown, *Essentialism: The Disciplined Pursuit of Less* (New York: Currency, 2014), 89.

63 McKeown, *Essentialism*, 87.

64 McKeown, *Essentialism*, 94.

65 Jake Adelstein, "Japan Is Literally Working Itself to Death: How Can It Stop?," *Forbes*, accessed June 2, 2019, https://www.forbes.com/sites/adelsteinjake/2017/10/30/japan-is-literally-working-itself-to-death-how-can-it-stop/ - f2511902f144.

66 Shawn T. Mason, Eli W. Carter, Chun Wang, Benjamin D. Goodlett, Richard Bedrosian, Janet Nikolovski, and Amy Bucher, "The Life Benefits of Managing Energy," Johnson & Johnson Human Performance Institute: White Paper, accessed June 2, 2019, https://www.jjhpi.com/files/JHPI34144 Managing Energy White Paper NEW BRANDING 1-25-2018.pdf.

67 Tony Schwartz and Catherine McCarthy, "Manage your Energy, Not Your Time," *Harvard Business Review*, October 2007, 2.

68 William Irwin, "How to Be 10% Happier: A Revolution in Mental Hygiene," *Psychology Today*, April 9, 2014, https://www.psychologytoday.com/us/blog/plato-pop/201404/how-be-10-happier.

ACKNOWLEDGMENTS

A THOUSAND THANKS TO:

Leith for *always* believing in me and *always* being game for whatever is next and for choosing love, life, and health. Let's keep going.

Matt McHugh for reminding me by the Owens River that I am the genuine article.

Morgan Snyder for walking the same trail in another valley chasing the same thing.

Sam Ainslie for teaching me how to play.

Alex Burton for living life on life together.

Jon Dale for that drive to Grand Junction together to buy a motorcycle.

Bob Stein for believing in me even when I was out of gas.

Dave Eitemiller for chasing after slide #25 together.

Chuck Bolton for flying here to be with me after I decided to eject on my career.

Chad Turner for being in the mire and muck with me.

Jack O'Neill for friendship and for writing the soundtrack of my life.

Kent Hildebrand for hiring me even though I didn't lie, cheat, and steal.

Ryan and Heidi Miller for dreaming in Penticton at Joy Farm.

Matt Toth for inviting me to own the atmosphere of my life.

John Blase and Jeremy Jones for believing in my stories and shaping my words into prose draft after draft after draft.

The McHugh clan for all of your love and enduring support along our wild journey.

Doug Ament (Coach) for being the drummer on this boat helping me keep pace and my eyes on this finish line.

Alex Field for asking if I had more stories to tell.

Mom for your love, prayers, and grit.

My Aberkyn/McKinsey colleagues for bringing love back to business.

Rob Bell for showing me how to be here.

Miles Adcox and the Onsite Workshop team for helping install new life-giving experiences in me.

Greg McKeown for making "less but better" a way of living.

Steven Pressfield for *The War of Art*.

Seth Godin for two decades of apprenticeship to become a ruckus-maker.

John Eldredge for showing me how to be a son.

ABOUT THE AUTHOR

AARON MCHUGH IS A writer, podcaster, adventurer, author, and career liberator who is learning to master a sustainable work-life balance while weaving the rhythms of play and enjoyment into his every day routine. He hosts the fast-growing podcast "Work Life Play," leads Reboot Your Life experiential weekends, speaks widely, and is an affiliate advisor to McKinsey & Co., helping drive large culture transformations in North America.